The original Coalwood Rocket Boys (L-R Sonny (Homer), Quentin, Roy Lee, O'Dell)

The Rocket Boys of October Sky (L-R O'Dell, Roy Lee, Homer, Quentin)

THE 'ORIGINAL ROCKET BOYS' AND THE 'MOVIE ROCKET BOYS' OF OCTOBER SKY

FROM ROCKET BOYS TO OCTOBER SKY

Homer Hickam Books
Rocket Boys Publishers
Huntsville, Alabama

ISBN-13:978-1492746591
ISBN-10:1492746592

Front Cover Design by Evan Twohy
Back Cover Design by Linda Terry Hickam

September, 2013

*To Andrew —*

*Homer Hickam*

# From Rocket Boys

## to

# October Sky

*How the Classic Memoir Rocket Boys Was Written and the Hit Movie October Sky Was Made*

by

**Homer Hickam**

ROCKET BOYS

OCTOBER SKY

HOMER HICKAM BOOKS
ROCKET BOYS PUBLISHERS
HUNTSVILLE, ALABAMA

FROM ROCKET BOYS TO OCTOBER SKY

**1**

Until events conspired for me to write *Rocket Boys: A Memoir,* I had no idea the story of my boyhood life in the West Virginia coalfields would interest anyone. I certainly had no reason to believe a story of those nearly forgotten days would cause Hollywood to pay attention. Yet, every day I receive a pile of letters and emails testifying to the continuing popularity of *Rocket Boys* and also the motion picture titled *October Sky.* But how did the book get written and the movie get made? Considering how many things had to line up perfectly, I can only conclude I am the beneficiary of a miracle, the kind most authors can only dream about coming their way.

For those who don't know the story of the Rocket Boys of Coalwood, West Virginia, here's a brief retelling. In 1957, the Soviet Union launched the world's first space satellite, which everybody called *Sputnik.* This caused a panic in the United States because the little beeping orb proved we'd fallen behind our dangerous enemy, the evil Russians! A space race subsequently started between the two rivals and kids all across the USA wanted to get involved. After I saw *Sputnik* fly over Coalwood, I was so impressed I decided to get into the rocket business. The problem with that was Coalwood boys were expected to mostly care about football and coal mining. Also, my father, the superintendent of the coal mine (the reason for Coalwood's existence) doted on my big brother, Jim, who was a high school football star. His second son—me—he wasn't so sure about. I was a four-eyed runt, a poor student, and apparently was not going to amount to anything. To imagine that I would turn into a rocket scientist was surely the furthest thing from Dad's mind—and everyone else's!

Ignoring reality, a specialty of mine, I recruited some other boys to form a rocket club which we called the Big Creek Missile Agency (BCMA), "Big Creek" being the name of our high school. When our exploding rockets began to stink up the town and blow holes in the mountains, Dad ordered us to stop. We didn't, of course, which began a fight between my parents that was hotter and brighter than any rocket we ever built. Mom was for us, Dad was against us, and the people of Coalwood were trying to make up their minds one way or the other. Anyway, they called us their Rocket Boys and, after three years of experimentation and many adventures, we went off to win a gold and silver medal at the 1960 National Science Fair. To celebrate and honor our teachers and parents, we held one final rocket launch at Cape Coalwood, which is what we called the old slack dump that was our rocket range. At that launch, my father showed up and he and I had a moment of reconciliation.

The *Atlanta Journal-Constitution* reviewer of *Rocket Boys* ended his piece by writing, "One closes the book with an immense feeling of satisfaction." It was like that in real life, too. I felt satisfied with how the experience ended, and it didn't take long before this time in my life faded from my memory. There were, after all, many other things to experience. I went to engineering school at Virginia Tech (where I built a giant cannon), then fought in the Vietnam War, then became a scuba instructor, and then worked as a NASA engineer responsible for training astronauts. Along the way, I also began a writing career and, in 1989, published *Torpedo Junction*, a best-selling history of the U-boat battles along the American coast during World War II. With so much going on, I didn't have much reason to reflect on my high school years in West Virginia.

The seed for what would become *Rocket Boys* was planted years before its creation. When my father came down with black lung, he had to give up being the superintendent of the Coalwood mine, but that didn't stop him from trying to run things, including my parents' retirement house in Myrtle Beach, South Carolina. One of the ways he did this was by pitching out anything he deemed not useful. This probably drove my packrat mother a bit crazy, but she played along. One day, shortly before Dad passed away in 1989, I received a dozen or so boxes with a note from my mom explaining this was all my "stuff" left over from my childhood and I could keep it or throw it away. Carelessly, I stacked the boxes in my garage and avoided looking at them until 1994 when water seeped inside and got them wet. Pondering the collapsing mess, I noticed that unlike the other boxes, which had my mom's handwriting on them, one box, a shoebox, was marked by my dad's crabbed scrawl. He had written but one word on it—*SONNY*—my nickname when I was a boy. When I opened the box, I found two things: the medal I'd won at the 1960 National Science Fair and a perfectly crafted steel rocket nozzle built in Coalwood's mine machine shop. I could only conclude my father had saved these things for me. But why? Into my head popped an image, the final day when we Rocket Boys had launched our last, great rocket. Dad had pushed the button that sent our missile skyward and then we had shared a moment of understanding. But what was that really all about? I wasn't sure, but on some deep level I started to think about it.

The medal went into a drawer, the nozzle became a paperweight on my desk. Just before Christmas that year, my phone rang and I found myself talking to Pat Trenner, editor of *Smithsonian Air & Space* magazine. I'd written a couple of articles previously for Pat and she had always liked my work so I wasn't too surprised when she said, "Homer, I need a short article as a filler and I thought of you. Do you have anything?"

That's when I looked across my desk and saw the rocket nozzle my dad had saved for me. "Pat," I said, "when I was a boy in a West Virginia coal town, I built rockets. How about an article about that?"

I have to confess that Pat was completely, totally, and utterly underwhelmed with my idea, but she graciously said, "Write it and I'll take a look."

Maybe the story had always been pent up inside me, or maybe the artifacts Dad had saved caused me to recall it. I'm not certain. All I know is I started to write and the words flowed out of me like a literary river. I recalled each of the five other boys who made up our rocket club, randy Roy Lee, excitable O'Dell, polio-afflicted Sherman, studious Billy, and genius Quentin. I recalled our marvelous physics and chemistry teacher, Miss Riley, and how she encouraged us to take our chances with the science fairs, and how my mom backed us up against my dad and how the town disliked us at first but then came to enthusiastically support us. I wrote the article in a few hours and faxed it to Pat. The next morning, she called. "Half the people in my office are laughing at your article, Homer," she said, "and the other half is crying. I think you're onto something special. We're publishing it!"

The article came out in *Air & Space*'s February, 1995 issue and can be found on my website under *The Article that Started it All* (http://www.homerhickam.com/books/other.shtml). Before long, I was swamped with letters from people telling me they wanted more of those feisty Rocket Boys. When I got letters from two independent movie producers who thought my story might make a good film, I knew I needed help. Although they seemed honest, there was always the possibility my story might be fictionalized or otherwise ripped off. But

8

where to go for help?  I didn't know anybody in Hollywood. All I knew was I'd better find somebody—and fast.

## 2

After I gave it some thought, I recalled that I did know someone in Hollywood after all. In 1989, after my first book Torpedo Junction was published, I was called by Neil Russell, an established producer who was interested in turning my true story about the World War II U-boat battles along the American coast into a movie. Nothing came of it, but I still had his phone number, so I gave Neil a call, and told him my situation. He reflected on it for a moment, then said, "Don't sign anything. I think I know an agent who might be interested."

About a week later, I got a call from a fellow named Mickey Freiberg who said Neil had told him about me. Mickey, I would come to learn, was a legend among agents. Nicknamed "The Cowboy," he was a relentless salesman in behalf of his clients. "Tell me about your property," he said, and I did. He was silent for a moment, then asked, "What do you expect to get out of this?"

"Well," I said, "Linda and I could use a new microwave."

This earned me a chuckle, followed by another question. "Can you write a treatment?"

"Sure," I said. "What's a treatment?"

"A treatment is just telling the story like it's a movie. Can you do that?"

I said I could and worked on it all weekend, ending up with ten pages that told the story sequentially including a descriptive list of all the characters involved. Within hours of faxing it to Mickey, he called back. "If I can't sell this," he said, "I shouldn't be an agent."

Quite frankly thrilled, I asked, "What should I do now?"

"I think you should pick out that microwave because you and I are going to make some money. And I hope you're writing a book. Are you?"

I was now. But what kind of book? The concept I came up with was to write a memoir that contrasted my boyhood life in Coalwood with my life as a NASA engineer. A lot of pages got written along that track before I realized it didn't work. Looking for a fresh start, I talked to Emily Sue Buckberry, a high school friend who was then a professor at Ohio University. After hearing me out, she provided me with some valuable insight. "Let Sonny tell it," she said. "I always loved that boy."

After giving her advice some thought, I realized she was right. The story should be told as if it was written by the boy who experienced it. But to do that, I would have to find that boy and get inside his head because, after all, Sonny Hickam wasn't me. He was a boy who'd never been anywhere other than Coalwood, a boy who'd not fought in a war, a boy who hadn't gone to engineering school, a boy for whom nearly everything in the world was something of a mystery. The search for Sonny began.

My work at NASA required long days so I got up in the dark and wrote until I had to go to work. When I got home, I ran a couple of miles to recharge my batteries and then, after a quick dinner, wrote until I couldn't keep my eyes open. Four or five hours of sleep a night became normal but it didn't matter. I was obsessed with telling the story and, to my delight, the little town of Coalwood started to come alive again. The miners, their lunch pails clunking against their legs, trudged up the old path to the mine. The people of the town bustled in and out of the company store and gathered on the church steps after Sunday services to gossip. My mother was in her kitchen, her refuge, in front of the big portrait she was painting of the beach and the ocean. My dogs, Dandy and Poteet, waited in my basement laboratory, their tails wagging at the sight of me. In my room, there was my old desk and the book my physics teacher Miss Riley had given me. Everything and everyone was still there, all in their places, defining the path, urging me along as I wrote.

And there was someone else there, too. He was silent, but every time I tried to turn away from him, he moved like a phantom to stay in my view. It was my father, standing on that old slack dump we called Cape Coalwood while our last, great rocket soared overhead. It was a shining moment in my life, but I still wasn't certain why it was so important. For me and everyone else to find out, Sonny would have to take us there.

FROM ROCKET BOYS TO OCTOBER SKY

**3**

Astonishment was my natural reaction when, just a few months later, Mickey negotiated a deal with Universal Studios based on my treatment with Charles (Chuck) Gordon as the producer. Chuck, Mickey said, had produced such fine films as *Field of Dreams* and *Die Hard* and had a solid reputation in the movie industry.

When Mickey began to go through the contract terms, Linda tried to take notes, but the names, rights, representations, warranties, and indemnities were coming at us like bullets from a machine gun. When Mickey told us the money Universal was willing to pay for an option to my story and then another much larger amount if the movie was made, Linda and I stared at each other and shook our heads in wonder. We had never imagined that we would have that much money, not that either of us had ever put a lot of store in being rich. I was making a nice salary as a NASA engineer and Linda was a graphic artist for a NASA contractor. My remark on the microwave oven reflected our simple tastes. We both had old cars which got us where we needed to go and our house was small but in a nice neighborhood. About the only luxuries we allowed ourselves were diving trips to the Caribbean. As amazing as the Hollywood money all sounded, it simply did not seem real and actually felt a little dangerous. I sensed the life we knew and enjoyed was about to change.

When the option money arrived, Linda and I bought a new microwave and put the rest in our savings account. Deep in my heart, I still couldn't believe anybody would want to make a movie about the Coalwood Rocket Boys, but then the phone rang, and I found myself talking to Chuck Gordon himself. He told me how much he'd enjoyed my treatment and then handed the conversation over to Marc Sternberg, an associate. Marc asked if I would talk to Lewis Colick, an A-list writer he and Chuck wanted to write the screenplay. "If we can get Lewis on board," Marc said, "that would go a long way to getting the movie made."

A few days later, Lewis called. He was very friendly, but told me up front that he was only calling as a favor to Chuck. He was pretty sure he wasn't the right person to pen a screenplay set in rural West Virginia. After all, he'd grown up in Brooklyn and knew nothing about small towns!

When I asked him about his boyhood friends, he described them as youngsters who liked to play in the streets. "We got in trouble at times," he confessed, "but we always felt safe. Everybody in the neighborhood looked after us. We couldn't get away with much because our parents would hear about it before we got home."

Picking up on that, I said, "Except for the setting, that actually doesn't sound much different from Coalwood. You had concrete streets and tenements, I had mountains and company houses. I bet you also wanted to get out of there as soon as you could, but now you sometimes wish you could go back."

Lewis laughed and agreed maybe I was right. We talked a little more and then, after cordial goodbyes, hung up. Mickey called a week later and said Lewis was in. "You did really good, Homer," he said. "Chuck and Marc are grateful. You're a player!"

Being a "player" sounded fine and I agreed to send Lewis what I'd written to date, which was about ten chapters or perhaps a third of the book. Before long, Mickey called and said everybody agreed the chapters were wonderful. He also had an interested editor at Putnam. This all left me feeling good about everything, but then, a couple of months later, Mickey called and said the editor at Putnam had passed on the book. When I asked what was wrong with it, Mickey said there was nothing wrong, that it was just the wrong editor. When I hung up, I was worried. The movie Lewis was writing was going to be based on a treatment and an incomplete book manuscript for which I had no publisher. Everything seemed out of kilter.

When I finished the first draft of the manuscript, I hired a college English professor to read it, asking that he tell me exactly what he thought and not to spare any criticism, regardless of how harsh it might be. His report was almost entirely extravagant in its praise. Linda and other readers also loved it. Feeling more confident, I decided the time had come for me to share the manuscript with the other Rocket Boys. Although they'd read my *Air & Space* article, this was the first time I'd told them anything about a book or a movie. Roy Lee, O'Dell, Billy, and Quentin (Sherman had passed away years before) all reported back that they admired what I'd written although none of them thought anything was ever going to come of it, especially not a movie. After a good laugh at my expense, O'Dell said, "Be sure to invite us to the premiere!" Roy Lee was bemused, wondering, "Sonny, who would care about what we did back in high school?"

I let the boys think what they wanted to think. For all I knew, they were right, and for months afterwards, it seemed they were. Mickey had no news on either the movie or any interested publishers. All I could do was sharpen the manuscript and ponder the main character. I still didn't think I'd found the real Sonny Hickam. Who *was* that boy?

One thing I learned writing *Rocket Boys* was that a memoirist must not allow his first memories to take over the truth. Often, such memories are the ones we've told ourselves to cover up the hurt and pain of what actually happened. Working instinctively, I kept peeling away Sonny's character layer by layer. Some of the things he did I understood but at other times, I was uncertain about his motivation. Then came the day when the boy presented himself. "Hey, old man," he said. "Stop putting words in my mouth and making me do things I wouldn't do. You write about me like I was an innocent boy, picked on all the time. Well, think about why my big brother wanted to beat me up. Did you ever consider it might be because I was a sneaky little brat who deserved it? Remember I used to put rocks in his shoes at night, down in the toes where he couldn't feel them until he'd jammed his feet in? And how about Dad? In school, I was lazy as a cloud in the sky. You think maybe that's why he thought I was dull? And after I started building rockets, you think I went to Mr. Bykovski because he was the best mechanic in town? No, I asked for his help because I knew I could get to him, make him feel sorry for me and all." He wiped his nose with the back of his dirty hand. "And that's what got him killed."

"That explains why you stopped building your rockets after the accident!" I said. "I wondered about that. You were ashamed!"

The boy I once was laughed a bitter laugh. "I wasn't ashamed. Something far worse. I felt *nothing*!"

*Nothing*! And there it was. At last, I realized what I had missed in the first draft. Sonny Hickam was sometimes sneaky and selfish. What he did with his rockets, chasing girls, and making trouble for his brother and his parents was just part of his many plans to get his own way, plans that often fell apart. Yes, at first he felt nothing when the machinist who'd helped him had been killed, but then he felt like his insides were about to explode. Sonny could be noble but it wasn't his nobility that made him an interesting narrator. It was because of how he'd been molded by the people of Coalwood and his teachers to do the

18

right thing even when his inclination took him in the opposite direction. He was always struggling!

Upon this insight, I thought: *Got you, you little rat! I know who you are!* Sonny just laughed.

Eagerly, I settled in behind my computer and rewrote vast parts of the book, this time bringing in the comedy and tragedy of the real Sonny telling his story. In the midst of the rewrite, Mickey called with an update on Hollywood. "Something you should know," he said. "They've decided to compress everything into one school year."

This was terrible news. The story had occurred over a three-year period during which so many things had happened that a few months couldn't possibly encompass the sweep of the story Sonny was telling. "You've got to trust Chuck, Marc, and Lewis," Mickey said. "They know what they're doing."

Whether I trusted them or not wasn't the point. I knew Lewis was still working off the treatment and the first chapters of an old draft. When I told Mickey I wanted to send them my latest, he said, "It would only confuse things. Oh, by the way, you're going to be called Homer in the movie, not Sonny. They think Homer sounds more West Virginian. They've also changed your dad's name to John."

I was still sputtering when he hung up. My dad's name was, of course, Homer. I was named after him. It seemed like a double insult for both our names to be changed.

In November, 1996, Linda and I flew to Kenya and then traveled on to Tanzania for two and a half weeks of safari. When we returned, my spirits were high, but they were quickly crushed when Mickey reported both St. Martin's and Pocket Books had rejected my latest draft. "They thought it was going to be a young adult book," Mickey said, "but now they don't know what it is. Maybe you ought to make it more for kids."

Confused, I sat down and read the manuscript again. What was I supposed to do? Simplify it? Take out the big words? Eliminate the struggle and sexual tension between my parents, dilute the lust Sonny had for the unattainable Dorothy Plunk, and the wiles of Valentine Carmina, who was destined to steal the boy's virginity in the back seat of her boyfriend's car? Was I supposed to take out Miss Riley's Hodgkin's Disease that was killing her day by day? Did I need to throw out Jake Mosby, the great womanizer and drunk who Sonny admired? Should I change Sonny back to being all noble again? After running these questions through my mind, I concluded that I wasn't going to do any of those things. This was Sonny's story and I was going to stay true to him and everybody else in it!

Then Mickey called and said it was time I met the people who were going to make the movie. Before going, I researched Chuck Gordon's life. The son of a furniture store owner, Chuck was born and raised in the tiny town of Belzoni, Mississippi, and then went off to the University of Alabama to gain a degree in history. After that, he'd headed for Hollywood where his brother, Lawrence, was already established. Chuck took his turn at being an agent and a writer before becoming a producer. Most of all, everyone who knew and worked with him described him as a good man who made quality films.

After I arrived in Los Angeles, Mickey picked me up at the airport and took me immediately to a posh golf club. At a table on the veranda, I was surprised to find not only the producer, but also the entire creative team of the movie: associate producers Marc Sternberg and Peter Cramer, and writer Lewis Colick. I took a seat while Mickey and Chuck joked back and forth about family and friends and the movie business, throwing out the names of movie stars and famous directors they'd worked with while I pretended I wasn't completely, totally, and utterly impressed.

When the time came to talk about the movie, Marc did most of the talking. He said *Rocket Boys* was an incredible story and everyone was honored to work on it. Peter chimed in and told me he was working with Universal to get a "green light" for the movie. This was the first time I'd heard the term so I asked about it. Peter explained that before a green light was given, a movie was considered in development, a process that sometimes took years. In fact, sometimes the green light never came. This was sobering information, but I appreciated Peter's honesty.

When it came time for him to talk, Lewis said he was determined to make the screenplay one that made my story come alive. "I know I will be remembered for *Rocket Boys*," he said. "It's as important to me as it is to you."

Chuck added if they could get a green light from Universal, it might be the most important movie he would ever make, high praise from the producer of *Field of Dreams*. I decided to stay silent on my concerns about the storyline in the script. As Mickey kept reminding me, I had to trust them. For the rest of the lunch, we all seemed to click, enough that I came in for some light ribbing. "We had to change your character, Homer," Peter said. "You're now a girl!" To my credit, I laughed.

Mickey told them how the book had progressed and his hopes for it. "It's only a matter of time before we get a publisher," he promised. Everyone agreed that was swell, but I noticed nobody asked for a copy of it.

About a month later, I found on my doorstep Lewis's draft script. Eagerly, I tore open the package and sat down to read it. By the time I finished, I felt sick to my stomach. The script confirmed all my unspoken fears. It was one stereotype after another. Coalwood was filthy, its people toothless and barefoot, the boys foul-mouthed, my father violent, my mother spineless, and the rockets were only in some brief scenes. A football game, not even involving the Rocket Boys, ate up a big part of the movie. Miss Riley cursed the referees and a huge brawl erupted with fists thrown and blood spurting. In another scene, striking miners were storming up and down the mean, gritty streets of Coalwood carrying torches. *Torches!* The only torches I'd ever seen in Coalwood were at the company movie theater when it showed *Frankenstein*. There was also a scene at the kitchen table where my mother worried about where our next meal was coming from as if we were refugees from *The Grapes of Wrath*. It even had me quitting school to work in the coal mine!

Linda came home from work that night and found me clutching the script in our dark living room. I'd been too upset to even turn on the lights. She sat down beside me and I handed her the script. "If they make this movie," I said, "I'll have to go up to West Virginia and apologize to everybody in the state!"

While I fretted, Linda read the script. "It's not that bad," she concluded, but I didn't hear her. I was calculating how long it would take me to drive to Los Angeles and somehow kill the movie.

"If you're so torn up, call Mickey," Linda said and I did.

Without interrupting, Mickey heard me out, then said, "You may not like the script, but Universal does. They've decided to hire a director. Your movie's got a blinking green light. Don't screw this up!"

I sat down and buried my face in my hands. Everybody in Coalwood and West Virginia was going to hate me and I wouldn't blame them. Then Mickey called back. "Listen, I'm working with an agent in New York," he said. "His name is Frank Weimann. He's got great connections. Give him a call. He wants to talk to you."

When I didn't reply, mainly because I was on the edge of panic, suicide, or homicide—nothing was certain—Mickey said, "Look, Homer, it's going to be all right. Lewis is a talented writer and he knows what sells to the studios. He wrote it the way he did because he knew Universal would like it. It's not the last version. Trust him and trust me."

22

At that moment, I wouldn't have trusted George Washington, but I hung up, and gave Frank Weimann a call. "Don't worry about the movie," he said. "Movies are movies but books are books. Your book is pure magic and I'm going find it a publisher."

"Thank you," I kept saying. "Thank you, thank you."

"There's just one thing . . ."

*Uh oh*, was my thought.

"I want someone else to look at it. To help you a little."

My morale, already plunging, went supersonic, crashing into my personal atmosphere and burning up like a meteor. "I'm a published writer," I said through gritted teeth. "Nobody helped me with *Torpedo Junction* and I don't need anybody to help me with *Rocket Boys*."

"Maybe not," Frank replied. "But I want you to talk to this fellow, anyway. See if you hit it off."

"No way," was my answer.

"Expect his call," Frank replied and hung up.

A sleepless week later, I got a call from a man who identified himself as David Groff. "I read your book," he said. "It's great. It could be published the way it is now. It could be better."

I allowed a long sigh. "How could it be better?"

"For one thing, there are places where you wrap up a scene too early and others where you go on too long. I could show you where those places are."

"I will not let anybody rewrite my work," I said.

"That's not my purpose," he replied. "My purpose is to point out to you what works and what doesn't, or if it does work, suggest that it might be even better. I won't ever tell you how to make it better, just give you my opinion where I think you should work harder."

"Let me think it over," I said.

"Sure," David replied. "Just let me know."

I thought it over, got in touch with my better angels (who were startled to hear from me), then called back. "I'm going to go through the manuscript again and then send you a chapter at a time. When will you be ready?"

"I'm ready now."

To my surprise, I loved what happened next. It turned into an intellectual exercise, mainly because I knew David was waiting to see what I'd written, and I knew his commentary would be on the money. Chapter by chapter, he became my touchstone, never changing a word, but suggesting places where my writing could be better. Together, we honed *Rocket Boys* until it was the best both of us thought it could be. Frank read the result, then called. "It's brilliant, Homer, and everybody up here is going to think the same thing. In fact, everybody in the *world* is going to think it!"

In the summer of 1997, a lot of things began to come together. Chuck Gordon called and told me he had the director. His name was Joe Johnston and he'd directed *Honey, I Shrunk the Kids*, *The Rocketeer*, and *Jumanji*. Joe had broken into show business as an artist and special effects technician on the *Star Wars* films and *Raiders of the Lost Ark*. In fact, for *Raiders*, he'd received an Academy Award for best visual effects. Chuck said there was no one more talented or perfect for *Rocket Boys* than Joe. By then, Lewis had rewritten the script and, to my relief, most of the West Virginia stereotypes, the football game, the torches, and the violence and cursing were gone. It wasn't the same story I was telling in the memoir, but at least it wasn't embarrassing. Although I still had my reservations, mainly because Mom and Miss Riley were weak characters in the script and it still had me quitting school, I knew it was best for me to stay silent.

In September, 1997, I flew down to Johnson Space Center in Houston to work on how we were going to train our astronauts and the

Russian cosmonauts aboard the International Space Station. When I got back, Linda and I had scheduled a date to meet at a small, informal restaurant in Huntsville. I met her there and was surprised to see her in a dress and heels. "I don't want to eat here," she said, "Follow me."

She got in her car and I followed her to a fancy restaurant called The Green Bottle Grill. "What's up?" I asked as we waited for a table.

She grinned and said, "Call Chuck Gordon."

I went to a pay phone and called Chuck. "We have a green light for your movie!" he roared. "It's going to get made! Do you understand? We're hiring people right now!"

I blanked out for a few seconds, but then stammered my thanks. Chuck said a few more things, none of which I processed, and hung up. I looked at Linda and then we hugged and danced in front of everyone in the restaurant, a few of whom applauded although for what, they didn't know. "It's really going to happen," Linda said.

"It really is," I whispered as we were led to our table. During the meal, I didn't have much to say because I was grappling with a reality that seemed entirely unreal. There was going to be a movie made about when I was a kid and about my parents and my friends and my teachers and the coal miners and all the people of Coalwood. It was crazy.

A few days later, Linda came rushing into the bathroom where I was shaving. She held up a phone and stage-whispered, "Joe Johnston!" Too excited to wipe the shaving cream off, I walked into the bedroom, sat down on the bed, and lifted the phone off its cradle. "Hello, Joe," I said.

"Hello, Homer," he replied. "I'm going to be your director."

*My director*! "Well, good," I said, gulping. "That's really good."

For the rest of the conversation, such as it was, I listened while Joe told me how much he loved the screenplay. He also said something else that was like lightning in the desert, a crackle of truth that split the air.

25

"You realize you've sold your baby to the slave traders, don't you? You need to accept that."

As his words sank in, I reflected on a lesson taught to me by the people of Coalwood. You take a fellow's money for something, he's got a right to do with it whatever he likes. "I'd like to come out to Huntsville to meet you," Joe went on. "What's your schedule?"

When I mentioned that I was going to Cape Canaveral for a meeting and a shuttle launch, Joe scotched the Huntsville idea and asked if we could meet there. This was fine with me so I also arranged for Linda to accompany me to the Cape. She in turn asked Bambi Ingram, an artist friend of hers, to come along so she wouldn't be by herself while I was at my various meetings. Joe said he was going to bring Larry Franco who was on board with *Rocket Boys* as a line producer. I immediately looked Larry up and discovered that he had produced *Starman*, probably one of the most literate science fiction movies ever made. This was encouraging.

When we met at the Kennedy Space Center visitor's center, Linda and I instantly liked Joe and Larry. Joe was a tall, lean, square-jawed Texas boy, Larry a bearded, loquacious fellow from Sonora, California. Although I was filled with curiosity about their plans for *Rocket Boys*, I didn't ask. It just didn't seem polite.

I had arranged for a "gold tour" which was an up close and personal look at the launch facilities of the Cape. Our guides were agreeable to take us anywhere we wanted to go, including to the pad where the shuttle *Columbia* was being readied for flight. After taking the elevator ride to the top of the shuttle stack, Joe and Larry were astonished at how close they were to the awesome rocket. Larry got on his cell phone and called friends. "You won't believe where I am!" he crowed. "Arms-length from the shuttle!

For his part, Joe took it all in with a tight-lipped frown, his arms crossed, his brown-blonde hair ruffled by the sea breeze. He was intently thinking about something, that much was clear, but what it was, he didn't say. I would learn later that this was normal for Joe. He rarely spoke without thinking about what he was going to say, his words like gold coins carefully chosen from a box and then handed out one by one.

One of the astronauts flying aboard *Columbia* was Dr. Takao Doi, a Japanese mission specialist and also one of my best friends. Takao was carrying a special cargo for me, my National Science Fair medal and a bolt from the Coalwood-constructed rocket nozzle. I passed that information along to Joe who thought about it a bit, then said, "I've been thinking about the ending to your movie. Maybe it can be you finding those things after your dad died or maybe you could be shown working here during a shuttle launch. I haven't decided."

Both endings were fine with me, but mostly I liked how Joe kept calling it "your movie" when he talked about it to me. It was respectful and I appreciated it, even if I knew very well it really wasn't my movie. It was Joe's movie, and Larry's, and Chuck's, and Lewis's, and a whole bunch of other people's movie long before it was mine. In the van back to the visitor's center, Joe opened up a bit, saying he'd once driven across the country to see a giant Saturn V moon rocket take off on one of its missions. He was clearly a fan of the space program and all things rockets. This shouldn't have surprised me. After all, he'd designed the iconic star trooper uniforms and the X-wing fighters in *Star Wars*!

The next day, we watched the launch of *Columbia* and everything went perfectly. Beautiful as always, she even blasted off to the second she was supposed to, a rare event in the history of the shuttle program. I took that as a good omen. After the shuttle had disappeared and all that was left were dissolving contrails, a small voice rose from the crowd. "Do it again!" a little boy called out. We all laughed and heartily agreed with him.

When we returned home from Florida, there was news from Frank Weimann. He'd shown my latest version of *Rocket Boys* to a number of publishers and they all wanted in. In fact, there were so many accolades for the book, he'd decided to put it up for auction. Over the course of the next week, the auction was held and the winner was Tom Spain, a senior editor for Delacorte, a publishing house in the Bantam Doubleday Dell Random House empire. I called Frank. "Thank you," I said. "It wouldn't have happened without you."

"It's nice to be thanked," Frank said, "and you're welcome."

I hung up and called Mickey. "Thank you," I said. "It wouldn't have happened without you."

"You're right," he said and then laughed. "This is fun, isn't it?"

It was now.

## 4

As far as I was concerned, the book was essentially ready to go to press, but Tom Spain was an exacting editor and saw some places where it could yet be improved. Under his sharp eye, I kept honing the manuscript. I did everything I could to make *Rocket Boys* as perfect as it could be.

Publication date was set for sometime in the fall of 1998 and Tom said I should plan for a big book tour. Principle photography for the movie was scheduled to begin in early 1998. This meant the movie was going to be made before the book was published. The situation seemed upside down. All I could do was go along for the ride.

At NASA, it was time for me to decide whether to retire or stay with the space agency and it wasn't an easy decision. After all, every day I worked there, I woke up thinking, "Oh boy! I get to go to work for NASA today!" I was also into some important and interesting work. My job was to set up the science and experiment training for International Space Station astronauts. It would mean a lot of travel to Russia and our European and Japanese partners, not to mention working closely with the astronauts themselves. It was tempting to stay and Mickey thought I should. "It's part of your mystique," he pointed out. "Most producers are interested in your background. They've never met a real NASA scientist!"

Of course, I wasn't a scientist, I was an engineer--a big difference. But I got what Mickey was saying. On the other hand, I seemed to be on the cusp of a writing career that required focus. The space station was surely going to suck up a lot of my time and energy. When I put it all together, especially considering I had 30 years of federal service, it seemed right to move on to a new career as a writer. I handed in my retirement papers at NASA.

When a call came from Joe asking for directions to Coalwood, I got excited, hoping the movie would be filmed there. Unfortunately, things didn't work out that way. After making a secret visit to my home town, he reported the light there didn't meet his criteria, explaining that the mountains around Coalwood were so close that a shadow covered it much of the day. He'd also discovered there were no hotels near Coalwood nor an airport so where the story had actually happened just wouldn't do. Although he would look at other places in West Virginia and Virginia, Tennessee ultimately won because Anne Pope, Director of the Tennessee Film, Entertainment and Music Commission, aggressively courted him to come to her state. Housing for the cast and crew? A working slack coal dump to replicate the launch range? An old coal town for exteriors? Not a problem. The perfect place for all these things, Anne told Joe, was the mining area around Oak Ridge, Tennessee, a town not far from Knoxville which had a big airport. When Joe visited it, he loved what he found and the wheels started to turn to bring the movie there.

The Tennessee folks also promised Joe sunny days, even though much of the film would be made during the winter. This turned out to be true. There were at least a dozen sunny days during the three months it took to film the movie. The only problem was all the other days were packed with wind, clouds, fog, rain, snow, hail, ice, and, once, while we all watched it bear down on us, a tornado.

**5**

Filming was scheduled to begin in February, 1998. Since I'd been hired as a consultant, I worked with set designer Barry Robison to make certain that every nuance of the film was accurate to the times. We talked and faxed back and forth and I sent him photos of old Coalwood and drawings of the rockets we built. Barry was mostly interested in what my house looked like, my room, the basement laboratory, the blockhouse at our rocket range, and Big Creek High School. When I dug through all the old photos I had, I was disappointed that I didn't have more of the Rocket Boys. For some reason, maybe having to do with the fact none of us owned a camera, we didn't take many pictures. The only photo I could find was one used for a story about us in the *Big Creek Owl*, the school newspaper, and the *McDowell County Banner*, a grocery store paper which, along with hamburger prices, had articles about local happenings. The photo showed us holding a mockup of a rocket, not one of our real ones. I recalled that I had brought out the mockup for the picture because it looked cooler than our real ones, but now I regretted it. To my delight, however, I came upon some ancient 8 mm film taken with a camera "borrowed" from my dad which included launches of our rockets. When I told Barry about the film, he got excited and said he and Joe would love to see it.

Joe was also asking lots of questions about my science fair exhibit so I forwarded him newspaper articles with photos of me standing in geek triumph in front of it. Fortunately, the photos of the exhibits also showed examples of our real rockets which were made of steel tubes, wooden nosecones, and aluminum fins. They were functional but not particularly handsome creations. When Joe called and asked what color the rockets were, I told him they were whatever color the steel or aluminum was.

His disappointment was palpable so I asked, "What color did you want them to be?"

"I was hoping they were white."

I laughed. "Now that I think about it, they *were* white."

To me, the color of the rockets didn't much matter and I was trying to be helpful. Then Phil Schneider and Whitney Kemp, who were in charge of props, came at me with an odd request. They said Joe wanted to know how to calculate the distance a rocket flew. "Do you mean altitude?" I asked, but the answer came back that, no, Joe needed to know how the Rocket Boys of Coalwood figured out how far a rocket flew, not how high.

I mulled over the request. The truth was we never cared how far our rockets went horizontally. Altitude was what we cared about and the calculations for that were pretty simple. We either used trigonometry (if we could see the highest point the rocket flew) or we used the physics equation $S = (1/2) at^2$ where S = altitude in feet, a = the gravitational acceleration constant of 32 feet per second per second, and t = time in seconds it takes for the rocket to fall back to earth. Assuming our rockets reached maximum velocity at launch—which the last ones propelled by zinc dust, sulfur, and pure West (by God) Virginia moonshine essentially did—then by timing the flight, we could come up with a fair estimate of altitude. Horizontal distance, otherwise known as range, was not something we normally calculated.

Then I recalled a time when we *did* care about range. That was when the State Police came to our high school to arrest us for a forest fire started by one of our lost rockets. The problem with their accusation was we had never lost a rocket and the rocket the police brought with them was, in fact, an aeronautical flare which Quentin immediately identified. The evolving movie script was apparently moving to tell that story, one way or the other.

I got out my old physics book and provided Phil and Whitney with the classic calculation for range of a free-flying missile. The response was positive. Soon, follow-up questions came in about the aeronautical flare. What kind was it and what did it look like? I wasn't certain of the manufacturer or model number, but I described it in some detail and faxed my answer back.

A new script soon arrived which included a dramatic scene where the Rocket Boys were arrested and put in handcuffs for starting a forest fire with an errant rocket. Although it hadn't happened exactly that way, I had no objection because it was a good, visual scene and I saw the need for such visual drama in film. Unfortunately, I also noted that the script still had me quitting school and going to work in the mine because the company refused to pay my father's medical bills. This time, I decided to send a note to Joe and Lewis about it. I kept my objections short and to the point. First, my father was the mine superintendent, a salaried man, and his medical bills would naturally have been paid by the company. Second, my parents would have lived in a tree before they'd have let me quit school. Third, the movie earlier established that the company was laying off miners. Why would it hire me? Fourth, I was only sixteen according to the timeline of the movie and there were child labor laws, even in 1950's West Virginia. In short, what was in the script was impossible.

There were a couple of jarring twists in the latest script that also called for notes. New dialog had "Homer" talking about O'Dell's dad having "his head cut clean off" in the mine. The problem with that was Red Carroll, O'Dell's father, didn't work inside the mine. He drove the town's garbage truck. He was also still very much alive! The script also made Roy Lee's father into an abusive drunk. In fact, Roy Lee's dad had died long before the Rocket Boys era and Roy Lee's mother hadn't remarried. I made my notes on these bizarre twists and sent them to Marc Sternberg.

Shortly afterwards, I heard from a Universal attorney who asked me to please go to O'Dell and get permission from him to have his dad killed off-screen in the movie and also get permission from Roy Lee to make his dad a violence-prone drunk. My response was that Universal should do it, not me, because I didn't agree with it. There it rocked on until Joe called and asked me to do it. He sounded like he was under some strain so, feeling more than a little bit like a rat, I dialed O'Dell and read him the line about his father losing his head. To my surprise, O'Dell laughed. "Dad won't mind," he said. "Just do what you have to do." Next came Roy Lee, who heard me out, then said, "I don't like it, but if you think it's necessary, I'll agree to it."

This is the quality of my boyhood friends. They were both willing to do whatever it took to support me. I called Joe back and said, "O'Dell is okay with it." On Roy Lee, I prevaricated. "Roy Lee will only agree to it if you make it his step-father." Joe agreed to that and another problem was solved although it still didn't keep me from feeling rotten about the whole thing. After all, this was about two men who'd raised me, in the sense that all the men in Coalwood raised all the children, and I was betraying them. On the other hand, in my defense, I didn't know for sure what would eventually end up in the movie. My fingers were crossed that these references would end up on the cutting room floor. As it turned out, both would stay in.

Since Oak Ridge was about a three-hour drive from Huntsville, I asked Joe for permission for Linda and me to visit the set when we could. Joe cordially responded that we were welcome any time and we could bring friends and family if we liked. He also asked if I could provide him with the book Miss Riley had given me to learn how to design sophisticated rockets. I had hung onto that book, titled *Principles of Guided Missile Design,* for all those decades and was reluctant to let it out of my hands. After all, it was from Miss Riley's hands to mine and that made it nearly sacred. But recognizing how hard Joe was working, I gave in and sent it up to Oak Ridge via Federal Express. When Cheryl Tkach, Joe's assistant, called to let me know the book had made it, I was tremendously relieved. Joe called soon afterwards and asked if I had really been able to understand the math and science in the book. My response was yes, but it took a lot of determination, time, and study. It was clear the book was also going to play a part in the next script revision. But in what way? Mostly I was afraid that it would make us look too smart. I was savvy enough to know that Hollywood, especially in the Spielberg era, loved kids to be smarter than their parents. Although we Rocket Boys had the mental tools needed to build rockets, we certainly weren't any more intelligent than our folks and I didn't want us to come off that way.

Then Tom Spain called with news. "Please keep this to yourself," he said, "but *Rocket Boys* has been nominated for the National Book Critics Circle award." Since I didn't know what that was, Tom explained, "It's big, Homer. Really big. It's like getting an Oscar. Just getting nominated is a huge honor."

I hung up, feeling pleased and validated, but it didn't take long before I started worrying about the movie again after I read in a magazine article that *Rocket Boys* was going to be a low-budget film. To me, this meant cheap. Looking for clarification, I called Mickey, but he was in New York, so I called Chuck Gordon's office. Peter Cramer answered.

After I read the pertinent parts of the article to him, he explained that a film's budget was whatever the purchasing studio said it was and, though he wasn't sure the article was correct, he guessed the amount they'd quoted of around twenty-eight million dollars was about right. "Chuck is going all-out for this movie," he added, "and he'll fight to see every dollar shows up on the screen. Don't worry." After I hung up, I pondered what Peter had said and concluded he was right. If Chuck Gordon couldn't make a good film, nobody could. On the other hand, I'd kind of gotten used to worrying about both the book and the movie, so I kept my options open.

With great anticipation but not knowing really what to expect, Linda and I headed to Oak Ridge in early February to visit the sets being constructed. Oak Ridge was a town created in the 1940's to secretly develop the world's first atomic bomb. Since then, the Oak Ridge National Laboratory had provided major employment in the town for engineers and scientists. The work in the surrounding area, however, was mostly farming and coal mining. On our first evening in town, Joe invited us out to dinner. When we entered the restaurant and sat down with him, he made a silent signal and, to our surprise, everyone in the restaurant stood up and applauded. It turned out he'd reserved the restaurant entirely for us and the film crew. I stood and gave a little speech about how much I appreciated them and what they were about to do. When I sat down, Joe said, "Most of them are sure this is the most important movie they'll ever work on." When I looked doubtful, he added, "I don't think you understand how powerful and inspirational this story is to other people."

He was correct about that. All I knew was I'd written a pretty good book that I hoped people would want to read. The next morning, Linda and I visited Rocket Boys Productions in a small Oak Ridge office building where I was surprised to find Joe's office walls covered with his own drawings of Coalwood and coal miners. In an adjoining room, a model of the town was on display. I shot some video of everything and then listened as Joe played the haunting soundtrack from *The Education of Little Tree* by Mark Isham. "I'm pretty sure I'm going to use Mark to write our soundtrack," he said. He also said he'd set up a visit to a local coal mine and wondered if I would like to go. I said I would love it and asked if Linda could go, too. "You're not afraid of going into a mine?" he asked her. "A lot of people have claustrophobia."

"Linda's a scuba instructor," I pointed out. "She's not afraid of much."

Joe shrugged and agreed Linda could go. For my part, I discovered I was eagerly looking forward to going underground again. I had not been inside a mine since my college days when I'd worked to help pay my way through college. I would later write about that in *Sky of Stone*, telling another story of Coalwood that included how I had finally found out why my dad loved coal mining so much. In fact, after being a coal miner for a while, I'd come to love it, too! That didn't stop me from wanting to work for NASA, though.

Joe went back to his work as we continued our self-guided tour, stopping to chat with Barry Robison, the production designer. Although we'd talked on the phone and faxed back and forth, it was the first time I'd actually met him. A slender and cheerful young man, Barry described his vision of the sets which included a coal mine tipple, a machine shop, the superintendent's house, and a variety of exteriors. The sets were primarily in Petros, a small mining town a few miles from Oak Ridge, and Barry recommended that we drive over there to have a look.

In Petros, we first visited the house that was being used for the interior of the Hickam family home. The owner was outside, watching the movie carpenters build him a new front porch as partial payment for the use of his house. When I introduced myself, he invited me inside. I was

roof bolts flashing overhead. It was all still so familiar. The script still had me quitting school and going to work in the mine to take care of the family after Dad got hurt but that wasn't the way it was at all. The real story was I went inside the mine because my dad wanted to convince me to be a mining engineer. When pressed, I had to tell him I wasn't going into mining but wanted to work in the space business which was a lot harder than quitting school, at least for me. I peered out of the tram and one of the miners watching us flashed his helmet lamp toward us which made me think again of that day in the mine with my father. I had written about it this way:

> The beam from his helmet lamp was in my eyes. "There's no men in the world like miners, Sonny. They're good men, strong men. The best there is. I think no matter what you do with your life, no matter where you go or who you know, you will never know such good and strong men.
> "You're my boy," he said and then turned so his lamp shined down a side cut, the lamps of his men flashing back from the darkness as if they knew he was passing. "I was born to lead men in the profession of mining coal. Maybe you were, too."
> You're my boy. In the dark, I could savor the words without embarrassment.

We stopped and climbed out of the trams. I warned Linda about bumping her head against the five-foot high roof and showed her the coal miner's walk taught to me by my dad forty years before—bent over, hands behind my back, head up so my helmet lamp shined forward. She emulated my walk while I listened to the dull clunk of helmets against the unyielding roof, the sound of rookie miners forgetting they couldn't stand up straight.

We also heard the roar of machinery. At a cut, a shuttle car trundled by carrying coal from the face—where the coal is cut away—to a conveyor belt. I took a deep breath and there it was, like wet gunpowder, the smell of a coal mine. Joe came up alongside and I pointed at a roof bolt and told him how it was used to hold the roof in place. I looked around and found a small pry bar and also showed him how tapping on the roof could tell an experienced miner its condition. A solid *thunk* meant it was strong but a noise like rattling dishes meant a fragmented, dangerous roof.

"Was that what happened when Mr. Bykovski got killed?" Joe asked.

"That was a methane explosion," I replied and then explained how the night of the accident, the ventilation fans had gone down because of a thunderstorm which had then led to a build-up of methane and an explosion.

When the safety man walked up and urgently whispered in Joe's ear, he immediately walked away with him. Wondering what had happened, I followed. At the trams, I heard a woman crying. It was Teresa, the assistant director. Her face was in her hands, her shoulders shaking as she wept. "I just can't do this," she said.

"I'll take you out, ma'am," the safety man said in a kind voice and climbed in, turned the tram around, and headed for the surface. Linda, walking up, said, "I guess she didn't want to see rats at the face."

I guessed she didn't, either, but I didn't take it as a sign of cowardice or anything else but what it was. Some people simply can't stand being underground. It's as if the mountain above mentally crushes them. Growing up in a coal town, I'd seen more than one strong man unable to withstand the trauma of working beneath a billion tons of rock.

Linda and I caught up with the group at the face. We didn't see any rats but we saw a continuous mining machine being operated by a miner named Squirrel. He showed me the controls, not much different from the ones I'd used when I'd worked in the mine nearly forty years before, and I took over for a cut. Linda crept up to the front of the big

41

machine, watching intently as I took a run at the layer of bituminous coal. I saw her look up, then edge back. When I joined her, she said, "I remembered in your book where you said it wasn't safe to go under an unsupported roof. That's why I didn't get any closer." Smart girl and she was absolutely right. A lot of good miners have forgotten that and lost their lives but Linda had remembered. She was also having fun. Any woman who has fun in a coal mine has got to be a good woman. She later reported that it took several washings to get the coal out of her blonde hair.

After we came out of the mine, Joe said, "Next week, we start filming. Are you coming up?"

After I said I would if he needed me, Larry took me aside and said it probably wasn't a good idea because the first week of filming was always prone to delays. That sounded reasonable so I told Joe I'd come up in a couple of weeks because I had marketing work to do for Delacorte Press, which happened to be true.

Before we left to drive back to Huntsville, Linda and I accepted an invitation to meet some of the actors in the movie. It was also a chance to see an old friend. Weeks earlier, Larry had asked me about the West Virginia dialect for his actors and I'd suggested he hire Emily Sue Buckberry, the high school classmate who'd suggested I go looking for "Sonny" to tell the story, and who also happened to be a speech therapy professor at the University of Ohio. Happily, Larry took me up on the suggestion, so we headed over to an Oak Ridge hotel where Emily Sue was holding a dialect class for the four young actors playing the Rocket Boys. After Emily Sue and I exchanged hugs, Larry introduced the four young men. Chad Lindberg, a tall youth with Jimmy Stewart looks, was playing Sherman O'Dell, a character that combined O'Dell Carroll and Sherman Siers. In the book, O'Dell is excitable and filled with energy while Sherman, who had polio and a severe limp, was thoughtful and reserved. I thought it would be interesting to see how Chad would combine two such diametrically opposite characters into one.

Will Lee Scott, playing Roy Lee Cooke, was small in stature but exuded toughness and maturity which was perfect for the boy who loved the girls and did his level best to show me a pathway through the strange corridors of teen-aged love. Chris Owen was Quentin Wilson, the genius of our group who also lived a desperate life of poverty he tried to keep hidden. With his shock of red hair and goofy expressions, Chris didn't look much like the real Quentin who was sharp-nosed and had slick black hair, but I could see why he was cast. He had about him the air of the quintessential nerd.

As for Billy Rose, the sixth Rocket Boy, his character had unfortunately been eliminated from the script. I hated that he wasn't going to be in the movie but I understood why. For one thing, four actors were cheaper than six. For another, to develop six boys would require time and time is always the enemy in any movie. I had never argued about this aspect of the script. As a writer, I fully understood why it had been done although I felt bad for Billy.

Last to be introduced was Jake Gyllenhaal who was playing me, or at least the Hollywood version of Sonny/Homer. Jake was a handsome young man—sixteen at the time and still in high school—with deep blue eyes (mine are brown) that twinkled with mischief. He vigorously shook my hand. "I hope I can do you justice," he said.

"I think you'll be great," I replied although I had no idea if he would or not.

Jake frowned. "Man, I don't know. I'm terrible at math."

"So was I when I was your age," I replied, which was the truth. I added, "We can talk more about things later."

"That would be great!" he said while grinning a lopsided smile that I guessed every girl in the world would find cute. He seemed like a nice boy and I was glad he'd gotten the part. I just hoped he was a good actor, too.

On the drive home, I kept thinking about the actors playing the Rocket Boys. All came with solid acting credentials except Jake who had little movie experience except for a couple of brief scenes as Billy Crystal's son in *City Slickers* and a small part in *Homegrown*, a low-budget film directed by his father, Stephen Gyllenhaal. Jake's mom was Naomi Foner, a respected screenplay writer. That meant he'd grown up in Hollywood where nepotism in films was rife. Was Jake really up to playing the lead role in a movie? I didn't know, but we were all about to find out.

## 6

Linda and I returned to the set the second week of filming. The first scene we saw was outdoors. The weather was pleasantly crisp, the location a small wooded hill near a narrow, winding country road. Joe was smiling because he was getting all the sunlight he could handle. Somebody handed me a script for the day's shooting and I stepped aside to devour it. Immediately, I saw the scene was a nod toward a character in my memoir named Jake Mosby. Mosby, a junior engineer, was an important mentor for the boys, teaching them lessons on trigonometry and life. He was also a flawed character who owned a red Corvette in which he often roared drunkenly through Coalwood with a series of girlfriends. Although there was a character named Jake Mosby in the script, he'd been changed into a mine foreman. Played by the wonderful David Dwyer, this "Jake" would be an important one in the movie but the Jake Mosby of the book was nowhere to be found in the screenplay except as an unnamed character driving a sports car in the scene about to be played out.

The setup required Roy Lee, disgusted because his old car has broken down again, to shoot at it with a rifle while the other boys watch. After the car is satisfactorily bullet-riddled, the boys get into an argument about their future. I liked the initial lines where Homer tells the other boys he doesn't understand why they want to act like a bunch of hillbillies. Roy Lee replies, "I got some bad news for you, Homer. We

FROM ROCKET BOYS TO OCTOBER SKY

*are* a bunch of hillbillies!"

The scene ends when a young man driving a Corvette—the nod to Jake Mosby—stops on the road and asks for directions while his passenger, a beautiful young woman, smiles at the boys. Homer gives him directions, then watches enviously as the Corvette drives off. Afterwards, he tells the other boys if they want to be coal miners, they can go ahead but he has other plans. The scene establishes that Homer is beginning to look past Coalwood.

When Joe called for action, Will delivered his lines with a comic flare. Whenever he moved, he made me want to watch him. Although he didn't have as many lines as Jake, I wondered if he might overshadow the younger actor's performance. When his turn came, Jake delivered his lines perfectly but I still thought Will had pretty much stolen the scene. After a few more takes, Joe was satisfied and an assistant director said "Check the gate," which I learned meant the shot was over. The phrase comes from the tendency of film cameras to build up celluloid debris. If no debris is spotted during the check, the film is probably clean and the scene can be wrapped up. No matter how the movie turned out, I liked that I was learning new things.

Will spotted me and walked over. "What did you think?"

"You were great," I said.

"Did it happen just like that?" he asked.

"Just like that," I said, which seemed to make him happy. I saw no reason to point out inaccuracies in the script to the actors. They needed to believe their parts.

That evening, Linda and I drove back to Oak Ridge to view the dailies. Dailies are raw footage with no visual or audio enhancements. For *Rocket Boys*, as it was still known, film was taken to Knoxville, flown to Los Angeles, processed, and then flown back. When I told Mickey that Linda and I had been invited to watch the dailies, he was astonished.

"They don't usually let outsiders watch dailies, certainly not the writer," he said. "They must really like you!"

I wasn't certain if they liked me or not but I was grateful for the chance to view the footage. Linda and I sneaked in and sat in the rear of the darkened room. The first scene we watched was one that had Elsie, played by Natalie Canerday, calling from a phone at the company store to tell Homer/Jake his new rocket parts—the original ones stolen—were on their way to the National Science Fair. Townspeople were shown crowding around Natalie with Terry Loughlin, the actor playing the store manager, yelling, "Give 'em hell, Homer!" It was a nice scene. After it was over, Joe, Larry, and Chuck conferred while Linda and I silently slipped out. Although I had been allowed to attend, I suspected my opinion of the dailies needed to be asked for, rather than volunteered.

The cast and crew gathered the next morning on a huge slack dump near Wartburg, Tennessee which was standing in for our Cape Coalwood rocket range. A slack dump is a place where unsold coal is stored until a buyer can be found. The actual slack dump we used in Coalwood was abandoned, the coal there only a couple of inches thick. The Wartburg location was an active slack dump with raw coal several feet deep. Almost immediately, crew members started coughing and complaining about headaches which I suspected was from the methane and other noxious gases seeping from the raw coal. A frozen wind also blew across the slack, bringing with it spitting rain and snow. Crew members circulated amongst us, handing out chemical hand and boot warmers. Scott Miles, the young actor playing my brother Jim, came over to say hello. His hair had been fashioned into a 1950's-style flat top and he was wearing a Big Creek High School jacket. He and I had a little talk about Jim and how he was one of the best football players in the state.

Although "Jim" was only in a limited number of scenes, Scott did a great job with his character. Whenever I watched the dailies, Joe invariably admired the work Scott was doing. He had a believability and ease about him that made him very watchable.

Jake's mother—the aforementioned screenwriter Naomi Foner—was to become one of my best friends on location. When Naomi said she wasn't feeling well on the slack dump, I told her she should get off it but she said she'd stay because she wanted to support her boy. As far as I could tell, the gas off the coal didn't bother Jake, Chad, Will, or Chris. They were having fun in their 1950's clothes running around atop the exotic material. Jake came over to me with a big grin and asked, "Did you really have a rocket range on this stuff?"

I assured him that we did. Jake wrinkled his nose. "It's nasty," he said, pointing at his shoes which were coated with ebony grime.

"Now, you're a real Coalwood boy," I said, which made him laugh. I could tell he had more questions but before he could voice them, he was called to makeup. Having your hair combed and lipstick applied by a pretty woman wasn't much like being a Coalwood boy but it was all part of the movie process.

Fred Murphy was director of photography. "Joe likes what Fred does with light," one of the crew told me, reinforcing my opinion that our director had a special concern with the quality of light in his movies. At the slack dump was a big boom to be used for what is called a crane shot. When Fred saw my interest, he explained how it allowed the camera to be remotely raised, lowered, and tilted. Fred had sold Joe on the idea of a crane shot to film the boys as they arrived at Cape Coalwood, a key moment in the movie. To accomplish this vision, a boom had to be rented and transported to the Tennessee countryside, an expensive requirement. That also meant Chuck Gordon had to approve it.

By then, Chuck was in Tennessee almost permanently. Every time I saw him, it seemed he had a cell phone at his ear. I didn't deliberately listen in but whenever Chuck walked by within earshot, he was usually talking to someone about what the movie needed and explaining why. Often, he ended the conversation with a rising voice, then shoved the phone in his coat pocket and, with his head down, stalked away. One of the many things I was learning was that a producer's job was to fight and scratch for the money to make the movie as good as it could be. Misty Cooper, Chuck's assistant, said that Chuck was battling with the penny pinchers at Universal Studios. This explained why he was no longer the relaxed man I'd met in California.

Occasionally, maybe just to make me feel like I was helping, I was asked for advice by the crew. For instance, the prop folks brought by a box of tools that the Rocket Boys carried to Cape Coalwood and asked me if it included everything they needed. Pawing through the box, I noted they'd put in a rolling pin, spoons, tin snips, a coil of wire, some wooden nose cones, fuses, matches, pliers, and screw drivers. I pronounced it perfect and they went away happy.

As February turned to March, it kept getting colder and wetter. Most of the cast and crew had gone to the Oak Ridge Wal-Mart and were decked out in colorful ski jackets or overcoats. The quality of Wal-Mart's boot selection was a big topic of discussion. Joe kept grimacing and clapping his gloved hands together and peering at the dirty gray sky. I was pretty certain it wasn't the cold that bothered him but the watery light.

While the rest of us shivered and waited, the Rocket Boys actors often played hacky sack. Chad with his long legs was pretty good at it and so was Chris, a grin splitting his impish face as he bounced the little sack around on his shoes. Will invariably only did a few kicks before trotting off to tell jokes to the grips, gaffers, and Teamsters standing around the heaters. Laughter followed him wherever he went. Jake was more interested in what the camera people were doing and the set designers. A lot of eyes followed Jake wherever he went. He had charisma by the bucketful but I still wondered if he was going to be able to bring to his role what was needed. Did a boy from Hollywood have the experiences to draw from to play a boy from the coalfields? After all, if he couldn't convince audiences he was a West Virginia miner's kid, everything Joe, Chuck and everybody else was doing would be for nothing.

Jake also took time to shake hands with the extras playing Coalwood citizens. His parents had clearly raised a well-mannered young man. Some of the crew flattered me by saying that the photos of me when I was in high school looked a lot like Jake but I laughed and told them if I'd looked anything like Jake Gyllenhaal when I was in high school, my book would have been titled *Rocket Boys and Girls*!

When everything was ready for the first Cape Coalwood scene, I picked a vantage point on a small hill and watched Joe's movie battalion go to war. After the four Rocket Boys were in position, Joe studied a video monitor, then ordered Fred to take the camera through its trajectory. Satisfied with what he saw, he frowned at the leaden sky one last time and then yelled, "And . . . Action!" For most of us strap-hangers on the periphery, his words had the opposite meaning—inaction, no talking, no movement lest we ruin the shot.

The scene unfolded. The boys climbed up a mound of coal, the boom camera tracking them as they lurched ahead. At the top, the other boys stopped and peered at the ebony wasteland while Jake raced ahead. "I mean it's perfect," he yelled, "We could build a blockhouse over there . . . and a launch pad . . . and we could even build a test stand!

Jake played the scene with a lot of energy and Joe barked "Cut!" After checking the monitors, he said, "That was perfect. Let's do it again."

The boys went back down the mound of slack to redo the scene while the crew scurried to reset the cameras and reflective screens. Larry

Franco joined me and explained why Joe would care to reshoot a "perfect" scene. The more shots, Larry said, the more choices during the edit phase of the film. The sky in the meantime turned ever more sullen, the clouds lowering until they seemed balanced on our heads. Joe glared at them and pushed a lock of hair from his forehead, a gesture I knew meant he was not pleased. "And. . . Action!" he called and the boys started up the hill again but Joe stopped them before they got halfway up. "Go back down!" he shouted, then shook his head and conferred with Fred. After he called "Action" again, the boys started up just as a shadow from an especially dense cloud fell across them. "Cut! Get back down the hill! Come on. Hurry up!"

By then, my feet were like lumps of ice and I knew the boys, dressed in light clothing and shoes, were freezing. Hot chocolate was being handed out by TomKats, the craft services contractor, and I gratefully took a cup. The servers, however, kept clear of Joe and the working party clustered around the cameras. The boys, back at the base of the hill, also didn't get anything and were visibly shivering. Joe kept looking at the sky and conferring with Fred. After checking the light meter and the monitor again, Joe suddenly called "Action!" Caught unawares, the boys hesitated before starting up which made Joe tear off his headphones and stalk out to them while everybody tried to look otherwise occupied. When he finished saying what he had to say, he tromped back to the cameras and the next time he called for action, the boys didn't hesitate. Up the hill they went and just as they reached the crest, the clouds suddenly parted and the sun burst forth in sweet, golden brilliance. Joe yelled, "Cut!" and the clouds, as if on cue, slammed shut. "Perfect," Joe said to Fred who nodded in agreement. For their part, Jake and the other boys just looked relieved.

The crew rushed to prepare the next shot. This one required the boys to fly the flag of the Coalwood Missile Agency (it was actually called the Big Creek Missile Agency). Joe arranged them like the Marines raising the flag on Iwo Jima and checked the sky again. "This light is going to play hell during edit," I heard one of the assistant directors say.

Naomi was standing beside me. "Joe got lucky on the last one," she said. "He's hoping to get lucky again." Before I could ask her what she meant, Joe called for action and the boys raised their flag just as the clouds opened a tiny hole that unleashed a streak of light that fully lit the scene. Joe smiled. "Check the gate," he said.

The gate was checked and the day's shooting ended. Although, as Naomi had suggested, he'd gotten lucky, I knew Joe wasn't getting the light he wanted. He was, however, a director who was also an artist who knew what to do with a gray sky pallet. In fact, what he would do with it would affect both the look and feel of the movie in ways nobody expected.

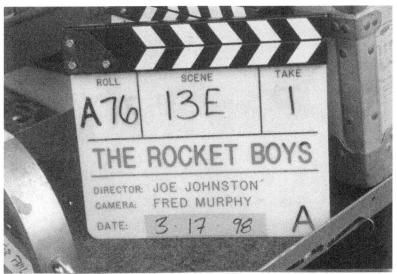

*A clapboard used in the making of the movie*

*L to R: Roy Lee Cooke, Will Lee Scott, Homer Hickam, Chad Lindbergh, O'Dell Carroll*
*Three of the real Rocket Boys with two of the actors*

*The actors playing the Rocket Boys prepare to pretend that they were knocked down by an explosion.*

*Joe Johnston and an assistant prepare for an explosive scene by donning safety goggles*

*Actors Will Lee Scott and Jake Gyllenhaal looking like dirty Coalwood Boys*

*Actors Jake Gyllenhaal and Chad Lindbergh rough and dirty like real Coalwood boys*

*Tom Taylor, a mine expert who kept the work scenes in October Sky realistic*

*The Teamsters loved Linda*

*Linda and I visit agent Mickey Freiberg in his Hollywood office.*
*L to R: Homer Hickam, Linda Hickam, Mickey Frieberg, Margaret Freiberg*

*TomKat Craft Services truck was popular. Actor Chad Lindbergh (C) with Producer*
*Chuck Gordon (R)*

*The real Elsie with actor Kaili Hollister who played Valentine*

*Mom and I look on as actor Randy Stripling autographs a copy of the script*

*Homer on the National Science Fair set*

*Homer (Sonny) at the 1960 National Science Fair*

*Jake Gyllenhaal being made up to look like a Coalwood boy.*

*The real Homer (Sonny) Hickam, 1958*

*L to R: Chad Lindbergh (O'Dell), Will Lee Scott(Roy Lee), Jake Gyllenhaal (Homer), Chris Owen (Quentin)*

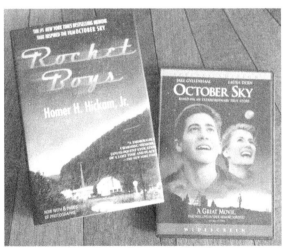

*From Rocket Boys to October Sky*

**All photos on set by Linda Terry Hickam**

FROM ROCKET BOYS TO OCTOBER SKY

**7**

The next time Linda and I returned to the shoot, the scene was when my first rocket exploded and blew up the fence around our yard. Rather than the heavy wood and wire fence we actually blew up, a white picket fence, unknown in the real Coalwood, was substituted at the Petros location. It was a complex scene in which three of the boys and the actress playing my mom interacted after the shattering explosion.

Earlier, I had asked Joe for permission to video everything and he'd graciously agreed. As soon as I was led to a place in front of the "Hickam house," my little camera started purring. Stuntmen, substituting for the boys, climbed into their harnesses for the scene. Attached to them was a spring mechanism to jerk them back just as the "rocket" exploded. The way the fence was situated, the mine tipple and shops could be seen in the background. That meant miners and townspeople needed to be seen walking back and forth and it was fascinating to see how all that was organized. The assistant director yelled, "Background," and the extras started walking. Joe waited a beat, then said, "Action!" and the fuse to the rocket was lit and the stunt men prepared themselves. When the rocket exploded in a mighty blast, the spring was sprung, causing the "boys" to be jerked backward. After Joe checked the result in the video that ran synchronously with the film camera, he pronounced himself satisfied with just one take. That meant several of the "rocket" props were left over. Mine is presently residing in Seattle's Museum of Flight.

While Joe and the tech crew conferred over the next scene, I watched Jake, Will, and Chad clown around with some impromptu dance steps. I took that as a good sign since their chemistry was key to making them believable as childhood friends. But Joe didn't much like it and sent an assistant director over to tell them to settle down.

Natalie Canerday walked over to say hello to Linda and me. Dressed in her 1950's housewife dress, she confided she was in so many scenes it was going to keep her on location probably from the first day to the last, whenever that was. It had rained steadily during the past week and that had caused several days of shooting to be lost. I steered the conversation to my mom, the real Elsie Hickam, and, by providing a few anecdotes, told Natalie what a strong woman she was. She thought about that and said, "Then I'll play her strong."

The scene that followed took several takes. Jake and the other boys replaced the stuntmen and sprawled in the yard as if they'd just been blown up. When Joe's call for action came, a prop man threw pieces of the fence on them and the boys shook their heads and rubbed their ears. Natalie flung open the screen door and came running onto the porch, there to see the carnage of her fence and the boys on their backs. "What happened?" she yelled with Jake responding, "Our rocket blew up!"

After a few more innocuous lines, Natalie suddenly turned on her heel and yelled "It's all right, Mrs. Beale!" at a neighbor woman in a voice that sounded like a wood chipper eating a steel bar. At the outburst, Joe's head snapped up and I thought he was going to tell her to do the line softer but then he shrugged which pleased me. Because of our little talk, Natalie had played Elsie strong and Joe was going to keep it that way.

Linda had asked Joe for permission to take photographs on the sets and he'd agreed as long as Chuck didn't mind. Linda asked Chuck and he'd said there was no problem. For the most part, I kept my distance from Chuck because I knew how busy and distracted he was and maybe I was a bit intimidated by him, too. In contrast, he and Linda were fast friends. Both were physical fitness and diet nuts so they had a lot to talk about, including teasing each other. I wasn't jealous, not much, anyway.

Between takes, I strolled over to talk to the Special Effects folks. Joey Digaetano, affectionately called Joey D, headed up the team. His two vans held a complete machine shop, stacks of steel and aluminum bar stock and cylinders, various chemicals, and a group of talented and skilled men and women who loved to fly rockets and blow things up. Just my kind of people! Although I didn't notice it at the time, Joey D looked a lot like a young Wernher von Braun but Joe had noticed the similarity very well. Toward the end of the movie, Joey D would show up and shake the hand of Jake after the win at the National Science Fair. I didn't know the scene existed until after I'd seen the first edit. Joe's response when I thanked him: "I wanted you to finally meet Wernher von Braun." One aside: To play the part, Joey D had to dye his normally light brown hair to nearly black. His fiancé was not happy about that since it hadn't grown out in time for their wedding!

Joey D and I talked over the rockets he was building. Usually, he said, rockets in movies were wire-guided but Joe wanted more realistic flights. He showed me how he'd scraped away at the motors to change thrust vectors that would make the rockets flip and turn on cue. It was a slick solution and I was impressed by his ingenuity. When the time came to launch the first rocket of the movie, he asked me to push the button. Naturally, I agreed!

The next day, we were back at the slack dump for a scene that included our beloved teacher, Miss Riley, played by Laura Dern of *Jurassic Park* fame. Every so often during the filming, it would occur to me that I was watching a major motion picture being made about a portion of my life and it would suddenly feel very surreal. Seeing Laura Dern step outside her trailer caused one of those moments. Because of something I'd written, this well-known actress had traveled all the way from Hollywood to East Tennessee. Incredible!

Everyone on the crew craned their necks to see Laura and, before long, a runner sought me out to tell me she wanted a word. Excited, I hoofed my way over to where she was standing beside an old car for the shot. After a quick introduction, she said, "I love Miss Riley. I didn't get a chance to read all of your book but I read the parts about her."

This was a nice surprise. I'd given Joe enough manuscripts of my final draft to send to all the main actors but didn't think he'd actually done it. Laura turned her dazzling smile on me like a thousand-watt bulb. "I'd like to talk to you more about her when you've got some time."

Well, what's a Coalwood boy to do? I kicked the dirt, grinned, and said, "Ma'am, just let me know when!"

After Laura did her scenes, it was time to launch a rocket. Joey D handed me the igniter and I waited for the signal from the assistant director. After a short countdown, I pressed the button and the rocket whooshed off the pad and headed for the sky atop a thin white smoke trail. Afterwards, more rockets were launched, some of them designed to be acrobats. One of them did a somersault, another ricocheted off the coal, another jumped a few feet, then exploded. Joe was ecstatic and came over to tell Joey D how much he appreciated what he and his crew had created. I added my enthusiastic praise.

With a lot of time on our hands while Joe and his camera operators and gaffers and best boys and such did all the work, Linda and I made friends with the drivers who, once they'd driven everybody where they needed to go, mostly stood around. Since they were all Teamster Union members and I was a former member of the United Mine Workers, and still just a Coalwood boy at heart, we got along great. They kept sneaking me fruit jars full of Tennessee moonshine, which I had no intention of drinking. I'd gotten truly sick on it when I was a teenaged Rocket Boy. To get pure alcohol for our rockets, John Eye the bootlegger in Coalwood insisted the real Rocket Boys drink a little of it. The result was I had never been so sick in my life. I wrote it this way in *Rocket Boys*:

> Roy Lee held his glass up for a toast. "To Wernher von Braun!" O'Dell followed suit and wiped his mouth, tears streaming down his cheeks. "Good!" It came out a strained whisper. Everyone looked at me. It was for Wernher von Braun, after all. I tossed back the drink, not even letting the liquid roll across my tongue. It went straight back to my gullet and caught on fire. I nearly doubled over as I felt it burn all the way to my stomach. I tried to breathe, but nothing worked. Roy Lee pounded on my back. "How about that, old son? Is that rocket fuel or what?"

Tom Spain thought the moonshine scene in the book was all-round wonderful and I did, too, but unfortunately it was reduced in the screenplay to a brief scene that only lasted a few seconds. I talked to Joe about expanding it but he shook his head. "I'm going to have trouble editing this movie down as it is," he explained over his shoulder as he walked away. I didn't pursue him.

Whenever Linda and I were spotted, crew members came rushing over to make sure we were comfortable with a good view of the action. The Teamsters all fell in love with Linda and kept coming by with gifts for her, mostly candy and cookies they'd taken from the TomKat craft services trailer. Her pockets were always stuffed with goodies.

Joe had his hand in everything. In one instance, we found a fellow spreading autumnal leaves around and it turned out he'd painted each leaf to match the colors Joe had specified. In the company store set, every tin can label was authentic down to the right color for the

Underwood Deviled Ham. At the high school set, we discovered each drawer in the library had the correct Dewey Decimal System labels on them, even though the camera only briefly panned through the scene. We also found a woman scorching and cutting a healthy plant that was destined to sit in the corner of the principal's office because Joe thought Mr. Turner probably wouldn't water it too often. We were shown the swatches of fabric and paint chips Joe had provided to the technicians to make sure everything blended in. The fellow who brought in the vintage cars confided that Joe had specified no bright cars. On set, Joe inspected the hair coloring of both the stars and the extras to make sure they fit his vision. He was also using smoke pots to give Coalwood a dark, misty atmosphere to match Tennessee's gray skies. This turned the movie darker than I think he originally planned but would pay off as Coalwood became an ominous place on screen. The audience could understand just by its pallet that it was a place to leave behind.

When it started to snow, Joe kept filming even though, for continuity's sake, Jake and the boys wore light clothing. To stay warm in-between takes, they gathered around heat blowers and sucked down coffee and hot chocolate until the time Joe ordered them back out on the slack. Shivering, Naomi stood beside me, her voice raspy. "I just hope Jake doesn't get sick," she said.

"He seems like a tough kid," I replied.

"Until this movie, I didn't know how tough," she said and went on to explain how much she and his father wanted him to go to college rather than become an actor. "It's opposite the way it was with you and your dad," she added. "You wanted to go to college but he wanted you to stay in the family business."

"Well," I replied, "it's hard to tell your dad you want to do something with your life that's different from what he wants."

"That's what this story is really about," Naomi said. "It's about you and your dad."

It shouldn't have surprised me that Naomi got it. A writer herself, she had stripped the layers of the rockets and the coal mining away from the story and gotten down to its core. *Rocket Boys* was ultimately a father-son story. *Field of Dreams*, of course, was also a father-son story and I wondered if this was why Chuck wanted to make the movie. When I next talked to Mickey, I asked him about that. "I guess we've all got issues with our old man," he replied. "Chuck, included."

Mickey, of course, was right. Our fathers had come out of the Depression and World War II, a generation not known for hugs or compliments. They provided their children with food on the table and roofs over their heads. We baby boomers had issues with our fathers growing up, only to realize what great men they were when we looked back.

When Joe came over to say hello between shots, I mentioned that Laura Dern wanted to talk to me about Miss Riley. He shrugged and said he thought it was always good for actors to talk. I didn't know exactly what he meant by that but I took it to mean he had no objection. Before long, Laura sent word for me to visit her in her trailer where she was having her hair styled for the next scene. When I entered, she nodded toward a chair. "How do you think the filming is going?" she asked.

"I'm not an expert," I replied, "but it seems to be going fine. I know everybody was excited about you coming."

"It was a role that interested me," she answered while the stylist worked her hair onto large rollers. "I could see layers of emotion in the character. Tell me more about her."

This was easy enough so I told her about Miss Riley and how tough, disciplined, and determined she was to see her Rocket Boys succeed.

"Not much of that is in the script," she pointed out.

This was undeniably true. Miss Riley's part was rather thin. Laura said, "I don't think that's fair to her memory."

A runner stuck his head inside the trailer to tell Laura she was due on set. "Tell them I'll be there in a few minutes." The runner glanced at me, then hurried out.

We kept talking about Miss Riley. Ten minutes later, the runner returned. "They say they need you *now*."

Laura calmly waited for the hairdresser to finish while I took my leave and slipped out of the trailer where I found Joe and Larry looking at me. A few days later, once we'd moved inside an old school in Knoxville to film interiors of Big Creek High, Larry asked me to meet him in Chuck's trailer. As soon as I sat down, his expression informed me he was about to deliver some unhappy news. "Laura's trying to rewrite her part," he said. "All she says is 'Well, Homer said this and Homer said that.' We don't want you to talk to her again."

"Joe said it was okay," I replied, as lamely as I felt.

"Talking's one thing but this is something else. You've been trying to rewrite this script from the start and we don't appreciate it."

I opened my mouth to argue but then clapped it shut. Larry was absolutely correct and it made no sense to deny it. I had wanted the screenplay to be closer to my book and, to the extent I could, had used a variety of tactics to make that happen. As for Laura, I knew very well she wanted to see Miss Riley's part expanded and I had helped her simply by talking to her. Considering the weather and the budget, things weren't going well and I had added to the problems of the movie. My response was to offer to leave and not come back. At this, Larry backpedaled, assuring me that he and Chuck and Joe loved having me and Linda on set. "We just need your help," he said.

"You have it," I replied and the meeting was over.

Inside the school, Chris Ellis, the actor playing Principal Turner, came up for a word. I was glad for Chris's presence on the set. It seemed when he was there, everything went smoothly due to his competency and fine portrayal of the irascible Mr. Turner. Then Linda came to tell me Iva Dean, Miss Riley's sister, had arrived. Iva was also a teacher and was thrilled that her sister was being portrayed in the movie. After we chatted for a while, Laura walked over and listened attentively while Iva spoke lovingly about her older sister. "I will do my best to bring Freida to the screen," Laura vowed. "Homer and I have been talking about how strong she was and I'm working to get more of that in the script!"

With Laura still on the hunt to make her part bigger (and better), I thought it best to stay out of sight for the rest of the day. My editor Tom Spain was visiting so we found a quiet corner and talked about the book. After watching some scenes filmed, he said he had his doubts about the movie but not to worry, the book was going to get a big roll-out. He showed me a long list of bookstores I would be visiting on the book tour plus television and radio shows that had already voiced an interest in having me on. Since there had been no book tour for *Torpedo Junction*, I had no clue about the amount of work the tour would ultimately require.

After Tom left, I went back into the school to watch whatever scene was next and inadvertently ran afoul of the movie makers again. The scene had Homer and Quentin in a science lab, mixing potentially explosive chemicals that might be good for rocket propellant. When the teacher spots them, they hurriedly wash their "rocket fuel" down a sink. A moment later, a student lights a Bunsen burner and tosses the match into her sink which turns all the sinks into flame throwers. It was a cute scene but it took a number of times before Joe was satisfied. Getting more and more frustrated, he kept calling for another shot. Finally, he shook his head and called for lunch.

In the TomKat lunchroom, I got a tray and found a seat. Joe came in and sat across from me and, without a word, began to eat.

Offhandedly, I offered a remark about the scene he'd just shot. "You do realize, Joe," I said, "that the chemicals the boys were mixing couldn't possibly ignite when wet, don't you?"

Joe slowly lowered his fork, looked me in the eye, and said, "You do realize, Homer, we're only trying to sell popcorn here, don't you?"

The rest of the meal was eaten in silence.

On the drive back to our Oak Ridge hotel, I told Linda what Joe had said. Her reply was concise. "Homer, you really need to just shut up!"

Of course, she was exactly right. Still, I pointed out that Joe and Larry and Chuck would go on to make other movies even if *Rocket Boys* was a colossal flop but I would have to live with it for the rest of my life. I had a right to make suggestions, didn't I?

Linda feigned sleep while I mulled everything over. What was right or wrong was not clear. The answer was gray, like the gloomy clouds that seemed to have permanently settled over East Tennessee and the people struggling to make a little movie about boys and rockets.

**8**

It was when we were the most miserable that I realized something remarkable was happening. This epiphany occurred during the filming of the coal mine disaster, the accident that killed Ike Bykovski, the machinist who my father banished underground after he'd helped us build our rockets. The marvelous Elya Baskin played Ike in the movie and did a terrific job with the part. The accident that killed Ike caused Dad to suffer an awful head wound and the near loss of an eye. In the book, as in the movie, the event occurs at night and when the injured men are brought up, it's during a lightning storm and a driving rain.

The scene at the mine was one Joe and set designer Barry Robison tried to make it as realistic as possible. A sprinkler system was brought in to simulate the rain and strobe lights were positioned to simulate lightning. That night, I was joined by O'Dell Carroll, one of the real Rocket Boys. Earlier in the day, O'Dell had met Chad who was playing him and they had enjoyed talking about what it was like in Coalwood forty years ago. Now, in the cold dampness and after so much excitement, O'Dell was unwell. "I need a place to lie down," he said. Worried, I asked if I could take him back to his hotel or, if he needed it, to the hospital. O'Dell assured me he just needed to go somewhere warm. I suggested the machine shop set, located in a small building nearby, and led him to it, made certain he was comfortable, and then came back to the tipple set.

Linda and I found a place in the shadows to watch the filming unfold. The extras playing townspeople, most of them carrying black umbrellas, closed in around sawhorses set up as a barrier and waited patiently to be told what to do. Joe, dressed in a yellow rain slicker, emerged from the bank of cameras and technicians, touched one of the sawhorses, then kicked it over. When Barry came running, Joe began to yell at him because the paint on the sawhorses wasn't dry. Everyone watched in shocked silence until Barry walked away with his head down. Joe, his shoulders hunched, kicked over another sawhorse, then returned to the cameras and his open-mouthed crew. The next thing I knew, Barry was standing beside me. He was agitated but he said, "Sorry you had to see that. I should have painted the sawhorses earlier but there's been so much to do to get ready for this shot." He took a breath, then allowed a long sigh to help him get hold of his nerves. "Joe just wants it perfect," he said, "because he knows you're watching."

The astonishment registering on my face would have been a close-up moment had the cameras been pointing at me instead of Jake Gyllenhaal. *Joe wanted the scene perfect for me?* I had no idea he cared what I thought, one way or the other. Barry walked off into the frosty night, leaving me to contemplate his words.

The temperature kept plunging until it hovered around freezing. A technician came by and said Joe was going to test the sprinklers with warm water so the actors would be more comfortable when they got wet. The result of the test, however, was a vapor cloud that cloaked the set. Joe ordered the next test with cold water and this time, the air stayed clear.

Joe called "Action!" and the rain machine started and Jake came out of the crowd of extras and said his lines as the townspeople reacted. After several takes, Jake's lips were blue. When he spotted me, he rushed over. "What were you feeling that night?" he asked through chattering teeth.

"Confusion, misery, and denial," I answered.

Jake blinked thoughtfully, then said "Thanks," and went back to work.

Joe kept calling for take after take and Jake kept persevering through them. Chris Cooper, the award-winning actor newly arrived on location to play my dad, stumbled with a bandage around his head through the crowd to a waiting ambulance. The townspeople turned away and fled the now-abandoned tipple while Jake slogged through the mud to the tag board where Mr. Bykovski's mine tag was hung, evidence that he would never be back to reclaim it. Jake had no lines but anyone seeing the movie knows by his expression and body language that he's cold and miserable and sad and in disbelief. It was not entirely acting since he was all those things after hours of being soaked by the sprinklers in the freezing, windy night. Still, I think it was the moment the movie began to belong to Jake.

It was midnight before the scene was done to Joe's satisfaction. By then, the actors and crew were nearly frozen but nobody complained. O'Dell came up to me. He'd warmed up in the machine shop and had watched the last couple of takes. "I have to pinch myself every so often that this is really happening," he said,

"Me, too, O'Dell," I said with a sigh. "Me, too."

The cameramen took down their equipment and the rain truck trundled away. The extras crowded inside the machine shop to get warm and have some coffee and hot chocolate. Joe slowly took off his rain cap, briefly looked my way, and then caught sight of Barry. He gestured for him to come over and they shook hands. When I saw him later, Barry said, "When you work on a movie where the director is just having fun, everything is pretty smooth. But Joe really cares about this movie and so does the crew. They'll do whatever it takes to make this film the best they can because the story they're telling is so rare. But I don't have to tell you that."

Actually, he did. For me, the tale of the Coalwood Rocket Boys wasn't rare at all. It had been my life, after all, but for everybody else, the tale was about a unique moment in time in a place that no longer existed. It was good to be reminded of that. I allowed myself a brief moment of pride in what I had started, then reminded myself of something the people of Coalwood taught me: When good things happen, it's usually because lots of good folks are working hard to make it that way. A lot of good folks were helping to make this movie the best they could every way they could.

And it wasn't because they were interested in selling popcorn, either.

I knew that and I was certain Joe Johnston did, too.

## 9

After the accident scene, the making of the movie shifted into high gear. The days started early, most of the cast and crew rolling out at four a.m. to journey to whatever location was on the daily call sheet. Most were lucky to get to bed before midnight.

A note on the extras who came out every day to be in the movie. Never in the history of movie-making has there been a better, more dedicated group of people. They had fallen in love with not only the idea of being in a movie but the movie itself. Many of them were former coal miners and they dressed up in the mining garb like the seasoned professionals they were. They loved carrying the old-style cylindrical lunch buckets although the prop guys had to fill them with rocks so they wouldn't swing them too high. The extras playing townspeople flocked to the trailers to get their costumes, makeup, and 1950's hairstyles. Their grins were huge and I signed lots of autographs.

Larry Franco worked with the extras on several scenes. At the beginning of the movie, a veteran miner holds a radio to his ear, listening to news of *Sputnik* as he descends into the mine. The gentleman, however, kept cutting his eyes toward the camera. Joe was on the verge of replacing him when Larry took the man aside and told him if he looked at the camera again, he was going to feel the effect of a shovel in the side of his head. The extra/miner got it perfectly right on the next take. Similarly, Larry threatened the extras with various mythical tortures if they didn't keep their eyes on the invisible rocket climbing into the sky in the last scene in the movie. The group mostly complied.

One of the best days during the filming was out in the Tennessee countryside in early March when the sun reappeared and the Norfolk and Western Railroad came to life again. All during my childhood, N&W trains rolled through the coalfields to haul our black diamonds to the outside world. To this day, the sound of a train whistle in the night takes me right back to Coalwood and the chuffing locomotives and clack of steel wheels rolling on the rails.

We soon learned Joe Johnston was a train buff. He lobbied long and hard with Chuck who in turn lobbied Universal Studios to bring in a steam locomotive and a line of coal cars. His excuse was because he wanted to faithfully recreate the scene where the boys are pulling up spikes and rails on a defunct section of track in order to make money to build their rockets. As I wrote in the book, the truth was we were going after the cast iron pipe beneath the tracks but never mind. The Tennessee Film Commission jumped in to help and the Tennessee Valley Railway Museum in Chattanooga agreed to send a 1950's era Southern Railway steam locomotive—old 4501—with several coal cars, all dressed out in Norfolk and Western livery.

The real Roy Lee Cooke turned up to see the train scene. It was great to see Roy Lee team up with Will Lee Scott, the actor playing him. Both of them were good at telling funny (and often dirty) stories and they soon had the crew laughing. After seeing Roy Lee and his wife Betty settled into director's chairs to watch the action, I moved in closer with my little video camera. By then, with Joe's permission, I was videotaping nearly everything.

The setup was two scenes. In the first one, the boys are shown stealing the track from an abandoned rail spur. In the second, after hearing a train whistle, they run to stop it from running off the rails. The punch line was it isn't going down the spur at all but past a switch on the main line. The first scene went well but the second required Jake and the other boys to run down the track. When Joe asked for them to practice the run, I noticed Jake had an awkward gait. During a pause to wait for a stubborn cloud to move, I called him over and asked him if he wanted to run like a West Virginia boy. When he nodded—albeit uncertainly—I demonstrated by running a short distance away and then back again. "You see how I held my arms? Tuck your elbows in and pump your arms with closed fists. That's how a West Virginia boy runs."

Jake tried it a couple of times, then said, "I can do that," and did in the next takes. These days, I notice Jake is a runner. I like to think I showed him how.

As for Joe, he was nearly giddy when 4501 chuffed onto the scene. I asked if I could go aboard and was given permission. Following me, with considerable help by a couple of stout men in the crew, was an elderly, slightly befuddled looking gentleman. He was greeted warmly by the engineer and the fireman, then allowed to settle into the engineer's seat. Joe was right behind him and I learned that the man was none other than O. Winston Link, the famous photographer whose series on steam locomotives had made him an icon in the world of train aficionados. I also learned Link was in the second stage of Alzheimer's Disease but on that day, it didn't matter. Joe was letting him fulfill a dream, to actually operate one of the locomotives he had so lovingly photographed, including those hauling vast lines of coal cars through the West Virginia coalfields of my youth.

Joe hopped off to supervise the camera set-up but I stayed on board. For the rest of the day, we ran up and down the track. Link's job was to wave at the cameras as we ground by while also pulling the whistle chain. When that proved too difficult, the engineer, who was actually operating the train from the floor, decided that he would also

79

reach up and pull the whistle. When Link kept missing his wave, I said, "Tell you what, Mr. Link. How about I pull your pants leg when you're supposed to wave. Would that be OK?"

Link nodded and I laid down on the cab deck where I could just glimpse the cameras as they came into view. When they did, I tugged Link's pants leg and he waved. When we stopped, Joe hopped aboard. "That was perfect!" He glanced at me. "You still here, Homer?" I shrugged and said nothing about the part I'd played.

We next returned to the Wartburg slack dump, this time to burn the blockhouse. In the book, the wood shack with a tin roof was torn down by bullies but burning it was more cinematic. Joey D and his folks moved a special blockhouse soaked in kerosene into position and then gave Jake and the other boys their instructions. To set it ablaze required Jake to toss a Molotov cocktail into the blockhouse from thirty feet away. The "cocktail" was a whiskey bottle filled with kerosene and a rag for a fuse so it wasn't like throwing a baseball. Joe came out from behind the cameras and had a talk with Jake about how to throw the bottle. I could tell he was worried. His star was about to handle a bottle of kerosene that was on fire!

Everyone held their breath when Will lit the bottle in Jake's hand and backed off. Jake didn't hesitate. He threw a perfect strike and the blockhouse burst into flame! While we all cheered, Joe maneuvered the cameras to catch the roaring inferno, then called the day's shoot a big success.

The next shot was an exterior shot of the Dugout dance hall between Jake and Kaili Hollister, the delightful actress playing the movie version of Valentine. The interior scene had been shot earlier in as near an exact replica of the basement dance hall I described in *Rocket Boys* as possible. This was another scene that Joe kept shooting over and over until he'd nearly worn the extras out. For my part, I was pleased that the song the kids slow-danced to was Tommy Edwards' *It's All in the Game*. It was the song that was actually played when my beloved Dorothy Plunk fell into my brother's arms and danced, her sweet head on his broad chest, while my heart broke into a million pieces. When I told Larry Franco that this was the song that I heard that night, his research showed that it hadn't been released until a few years after the Rocket Boys era. This forced me to do my own research. Happily, I discovered there was an earlier release of the song in the late 1950's. This is why that great old song is played in the movie.

The exterior Dugout scene was filmed on a back street in Oliver Springs where an old gas station had been painted to look like our teen hangout. Joe had decided to film it in the dark, meaning that everything needed to be set up and ready to go early. All day, the crew worked to get everything in place. The Tennessee State Police set up roadblocks but crowds of the curious still gathered as close as they could to the action. A neon sign that blinked *Owl's Nest*, the diner that was over the Dugout, failed and there was a lot of scurrying around to fix it without success. Finally, Joe said it would be fixed in post-production and the filming began.

In the book, Valentine takes pity on Sonny and seduces him in the back seat of a car after the dance. The movie version was much cleaner. Valentine is the same age as Homer and just wants to be his girlfriend. After the heart-crushing scene inside the Dugout, the script has Homer going outside to lean against the hood of a car where he grapples with the reality of losing a girl he never had. Then Valentine follows him and looks soulfully into his eyes. There's virtually no dialog but Homer figures out maybe he's been wrong about Valentine.

Joe shot the scene five or six times which didn't seem to faze Jake and Kaili at all. In fact they seemed to enjoy doing a scene which had few lines but lots of body language. Each time they did it, their nonverbal communication seemed to get a little better. I would later learn that a sexually graphic scene was filmed between Jake and Kaili but was discarded because test audiences didn't like it. If it could be found, my guess is the adult audience for the movie would love to see it as an outtake.

The next few days were dedicated to filming Chris Cooper's scenes. Chris, who was playing my dad, had only a short time to spend on location because of another role he had for a movie titled *American Beauty*. I knew him from two previous movies, *Matewan*, the story of a union mine organizer, and *Lone Star* in which he'd played a Texas sheriff. Poignantly, the last movie my dad had seen before his death was *Matewan*.

Before Chris came to Tennessee, I'd spoken briefly with him over the phone about Dad who he kept calling "John," just as it was in the script. It wasn't his fault he had the name wrong, of course, so I didn't correct him. Instead, I told him how proud Dad was to be in the profession of mining coal, and what Coalwood meant to him. He was not only the leader of the miners, but was also the unofficial mayor of our little town. This intrigued Chris and we discussed how my father resisted Coalwood's demise and took it upon himself to keep his miners safe. Chris asked if I had anything of Dad's he might wear or keep with him during the filming so I sent along a silver dollar Dad always kept in his pocket for luck, plus his wrist watch and his Masonic ring. On set, Chris always had those things with him.

My mother, the great and now late Elsie Hickam, chose to visit on the day when Chris played an intense scene with Natalie. Before the shot, I brought Mom around to say hello. Chris stepped out of his trailer dressed in the same kind of khakis Dad preferred for his work clothes. After I introduced him to Mom, he grinned and stuck out his hand to shake hers. When she saw he was wearing Dad's wrist watch and ring, tears filled her eyes, and for one of the few times in her life, my mom was at a loss for words. To her delight, Chris took Dad's silver dollar from his pocket. "You look just like Homer," Mom said. If this confused Chris since he was playing "John" Hickam, he didn't let on. Instead, he promised her he would do his best to play her husband. "Well," Mom said, back on solid ground, "all he cared about was that old coal mine."

"Yes, ma'am," Chris said. "I'll remember that."

It was a cold day so I gave Mom my NASA jacket so she could watch the scene being filmed on the Petros set. The crew rushed over a chair for her and there she perched, queen for the day. The wonderful actor Randy Stripling, who was playing the machinist Leon Bolden, the man who taught the Rocket Boys how to operate a lathe and build their rockets, came over to say hello. "I'm Leon Bolden the machinist," he said with a big grin. Mom puzzled over him for a few seconds, then said, "I'm sorry I don't remember you."

I rushed in to explain. "Look, Mom, there's the book reality, the movie reality, and the real reality. Try not to get them mixed up."

Mom gave me a warning look. "I'd say that's more your problem," she snapped and I knew it was time for me to back off.

Next, Natalie came over for a word and a hug. Mom looked her over and said, "I told Sonny I wanted Kathy Bates to play me but I guess you'll do."

Natalie didn't blink an eye. "Kathy would have made a great you," she replied.

Although Mom's remark to Natalie made me grit my teeth, it was just her way and, once they got past her directness, everybody loved her.

While Joe set up the scene between Chris and Natalie, I allowed myself a moment to enjoy the Hollywood version of Coalwood, noticing especially the sign that arched over the street that announced *Olga Coal Company, Coalwood, West Virginia*. When the extras, dressed in grimy coveralls and miner's helmets, moved across the grounds, Coalwood almost came alive. Mom didn't like Coalwood because it had ultimately killed her husband, but I loved the old coal camp. It was, and forever will be, my home.

The scene being shot after lunch was to show what happened in Coalwood after my rocket display was stolen at the National Science Fair. In the book and in real life, I'd made my first long distance telephone call ever, begging my Mom to intercede in a bitter labor strike in Coalwood so I could get more rockets built. In the scene Mom was about to watch, Natalie as Elsie strides through a crowd of angry, placard-waving miners to get to her husband's office, there to insist he settle the strike.

While we waited, I went over to Natalie and apologized for Mom, but she laughed it off. "That's a fine lady, your mom," she said. "She stuck up for everything and everybody she loved—you, your father, all the Rocket Boys. I love playing her!" Then she winked. "And I'll do a better job than that ol' Kathy Bates, she'll see!"

When the time came, Natalie indeed showed the Elsie Hickam spirit, striding purposefully through hooting strikers to the company office. After a couple of takes, the cameras moved indoors to the office set. There, Natalie barged inside to tell "John" to settle the strike or she was going to leave him. When Chris asked where she would go, Natalie raised her chin and said, "Myrtle Beach!" then wheeled around and marched out the door. It was a bravado performance. Joe went to Natalie and uncharacteristically gave her a hug. "Good job," he said while Natalie wiped away tears.

Joe moved the cameras in for a close up as Chris reacted to Natalie, his scowl dissolving into alternating pain, pride, and joy. Suddenly, Chris was my father, a man who tried desperately, but sometimes clumsily, to do the right thing for his mine, his town, and his family. Before the hushed gathering of film-makers, Chris looked searchingly into his wife's eyes, begging for understanding. That was when I stopped watching. It was too real. When I looked around, I saw I wasn't the only one who'd been affected by Chris's performance. Larry was wiping his eyes and Chuck was taking deep breaths.

Joe called a halt to the proceedings. Chris walked away from the set to be alone. Natalie went to her chair and bowed her head. For a few minutes, the hundreds of cast and crew and extras moved quietly, their conversations in hushed tones. Something magical had just happened and everyone was trying to absorb it.

FROM ROCKET BOYS TO OCTOBER SKY

## 10

Linda and I were on hand for three more big scenes, the National Science Fair, the "search for the lost rocket," and the launch of the "Miss Riley," our last rocket. First came the fair. The set that was built was astonishingly accurate, even including other entries. I walked up and down the exhibits, amazed at the care taken to get every detail accurate. I had shared with Barry and the prop guys everything I recalled about my actual exhibit and they had carefully recreated it. The first scene filmed was of Jake/Homer explaining a rocket nozzle to onlookers. Naomi, Linda, and I stood together on a catwalk above the exhibits and watched him go through take after take, flubbing his lines each time. The lines in the screenplay had been lifted directly from the book:

> When rocket propellant [is] burned, it first produces a river of gas that flows into the convergent section of the nozzle. If the river continues through the throat at less than sonic speed—that it to say, less than the speed of sound—it becomes compacted in the divergent section, bound in turmoil, and inefficient. But if the gas reaches the speed of sound at the throat, then the gas in the divergent section goes supersonic.

The problem with having those lines for Jake to say was they weren't meant as dialog. They were made deliberately complex because it was what Quentin and I had concluded from the study of our rocket book. I wasn't certain if it was Lewis or Joe who had lifted them directly from the book but there they were in all their tongue-twisting glory.

When Jake finally gave up and asked for a minute to collect his thoughts, I decided to go downstairs and suggest a rewrite of the line but before I could, Joe was pulled aside by the camera crew.

The next take had the same result and Jake was clearly getting flustered. Joe called for another break but Jake asked to try it one more time. This time he got through it except for one little stutter. Seeing how unsettled his actor was, Joe called a halt to the proceedings, promising to shoot it again later. He never did and it was this last take that was used in the final edit. Interestingly, it would prove to be an endearing scene, the stutter seemingly caused by Homer being awestruck by being at the National Science Fair.

When Linda's sister Elaine came to visit, we drove her out to a wooded site where a scene about the lost rocket was being filmed. In reality, we never lost a rocket, but I thought the way the scene was written made sense. The whole idea was to show the boys under stress and then doing what it took to prove their innocence. After using the equation for range in Quentin's dilapidated house, Homer and Quentin go into the woods and find their rocket. The first thing I noticed when I arrived on location was the boys were using a rope to measure the distance from the launch pad to the lost rocket. This, of course, wouldn't work in real life. Since, according to the script, Quentin and Homer used trigonometry to calculate the distance, the result would be the length of a flat base of a triangle. In other words, a straight line. Using a rope to measure up and down hills would be hopelessly inaccurate. "Should I tell Joe or Larry?" I asked Linda.

"No!" she snapped, so I shrugged and let the scene play out. Interestingly, I've never heard a word from a trig teacher about it. Sometimes, even trig teachers get immersed in a movie and forget reality, which is a testament, I suppose, to Joe's ability to put together a good story.

The scene required Chris/Quentin and Jake/Homer, unable to find their lost rocket, to come upon a stream. There, Jake squats as if to get a drink of water. Pondering, he asks about the wind and which way it was blowing on the day the rocket was lost.

A camera unit was down stream where a rocket mockup had been stuck nose down in the water. That was where Joe and Fred had set up a special shot where Jake would be in focus and the rocket out of focus but when Jake sees the rocket, it goes into focus and Jake blurs. It was a nice effect. Joe and Fred kept manipulating the camera until finally they were ready to go. Jake and Chris approached the stream and Joe said, "And...action!"

Jake started his lines, then fumbled them. I thought he looked upset and wondered if the previous day's flubbed lines at the Science Fair had unnerved him a little. Take after take followed and Jake just couldn't get them right. Finally, he shook his head and walked away while Chris, looking concerned, followed him. They had a few words, then Joe walked out to talk to them. They walked back, Joe to the camera, Chris settling into his spot, and Jake crouching by the stream. The camera rolled and the take was perfect. Jake caught my eye and I saw his relieved expression. I nodded to him and he grinned.

One of the most important scenes in the movie is when the Rocket Boys thank Coalwood for supporting them by hosting a final launch of their biggest and best rocket. It is also the day when my father finally shows up for a launch. An important scene in the movie, it was a pivotal one in the book. In fact, reliving that moment was the real reason why I'd written it and I was concerned that it be portrayed honestly in the film.

In *Rocket Boys*, the name of the rocket was *Auk XXXI*. Before it was launched, other rockets were sent flying, each one better than the one before it. The crowd was huge, people coming from all over the county to honor the Rocket Boys for winning their medal. In my telling, I built tension leading up to the final launch by noting we had never tried to fire a rocket of those dimensions before and we weren't completely certain if it would work. When my father unexpectedly showed up, I impulsively offered the rocket to Dad to launch and the entire scene changed from a celebration to a very personal moment between a son and his father.

Throughout the book, I not only craved the attention of my father but his touch. At the final launch, I had hope that Dad would put his arm around my shoulders and tell me I'd done something good. That would have been the payoff, and I knew the reader by then would be hoping for it. But I had to write it the way it happened which, to my way of thinking, was better because it was a surprise to everyone. After the rocket is launched, I wrote what happened this way:

> I was astonished to see Dad prancing along the slack, waving his old hat in his hand. He was exulting to the sky. "Beautiful! Beautiful!" . . . People surged from the road across the slack, following the other boys as they raced after our last, great rocket. Dad stopped his dance and put his hat over his heart. He bent over as if a great weight had suddenly been dropped on his back. He looked at me, his mouth open, and I saw in his eyes a curious mixture of happiness and pain that dissolved into fear. I went to him and put my arm around his shoulder, supporting him while he fought for air. "You did really good, Dad," I told him as a spasm of deep, oily coughs racked his body. "Nobody ever launched a better rocket than you."

Although I knew he was under a lot of pressure to wrap things up, I still went to Joe to discuss the way I had described the day in my memoir versus what was in the script. Lewis had condensed everything to just one rocket named *Miss Riley* and during its flight, the father was to proudly put his arm around the boy. I liked the rocket's new name but I thought my way—the son supporting the father in an ironic twist—was better than what was in the script. Joe heard me out, then said, "I think we'll film it my way, Homer," and that was that.

In some ways, the filming of the final launch was as thrilling as the real one back in Coalwood in 1960. I could tell the extras were pumped up, as were Jake and the boys. This was the climactic moment of the entire movie. Joey D and his team had prepared several "Miss Rileys," big rockets designed by Ky Michaelson, the famous rocket builder. I had one hundred percent confidence they would work. Joey D gave me the honor of launching all of these last rockets. They flew perfectly although I noticed a mild instability at lift-off, probably caused by the addition of a fake external nozzle.

With the rocket launches in the can, what had been a lovely day turned sour with the wind picking up and low clouds packing in overhead. When somebody yelled, "Tornado!" I saw a swirl of gray air drop from the clouds and start dancing along the edge of the slack. People started running while Chuck, Linda, and I sought shelter beneath a canvas canopy meant to protect the cameras. Another whirlwind appeared, turned black from the coal it was sucking up inside its guts, and hurtled toward us. With nowhere to run, we grabbed the spars of the canopy and held on even when we were lifted a foot off the ground. Fortunately, as suddenly as they had appeared, the mini-tornadoes vanished, we were dropped back to Earth, the clouds scudded away, and the sun came out. I heard Joe reorganizing his crew. Chuck, Linda, and I looked at each other and shook our heads. Without a break, the filming continued.

The extras, most of whom had hidden inside the vintage cars, climbed out and gathered in their places. Larry gave them a pep talk while also good-naturedly warning them not to look into the camera. If they did, he said, he was going to dock their pay. This was a laugh line as their pay was minimal. Many came up and told me they were extras just for the honor of being in my movie. In fact, I was the one who was honored by their loyalty and hard work.

Jake had a little speech to make and nailed it the first time. Then the cameras turned toward the crowd of extras. As they parted, Chris Cooper appeared, his expression that of a man who was doing his reluctant duty. This subtly changed to one of quiet interest as he was offered the firing box with Jake saying "This one's yours, Dad, if you want it." Over the next few hours, Joe shot the scene again and again. Each time, Chris put his arm around Jake's shoulders and the crowd reacted with awe as the huge "Miss Riley" flew aloft. Chris Owen got in the final line and it was a good one. "Watch it go, Homer. This one's going for miles." I thought it was the pitch-perfect way to end the movie but Joe had a surprise for me. After the "Miss Riley" scene, he would insert the dramatic, rumbling launch of a space shuttle followed by ancient eight millimeter film of each of the Rocket Boys, my parents, and Miss Riley. I can't watch that ending without tears in my eyes, no matter how many times I've seen it. Fans of the movie also tell me how much they love it when Chris Cooper puts his arm around Jake Gyllenhaal and many a strong man has confessed to weeping during that scene. Maybe Joe and Lewis knew what they were doing, after all.

The shooting day ended and the big tractor trailers holding all the lights and sound equipment and cameras rolled away. Since this was the last time I would be on location, I drove back to Petros, its streets now empty of actors, crews, and extras. The tipple set loomed, heralded by the arched *Olga Coal Company* sign. Someone had left a folding chair so I sat down in it and absorbed for one last time all the work that had been done to recreate Coalwood. A dog barked in the distance and, overhead, the stars blinked on, one by one. For just a moment, I was back in Coalwood again, back to the ancient place where once, as I described it in the final paragraph of the memoir, *"There were rockets that leapt into the air, propelled not by physics but by the vibrant love of an honorable people, and the instruction of a dear teacher, and the dreams of boys.^"*

Glancing skyward, I did not see a space satellite streaking across the starry sky. That would have been a little too perfect. Instead, I simply rose from the chair and headed for my car, not bothering to look back. I was instead looking forward to what was going to happen next. Of course, what I thought was going to happen was nothing like what actually did.

## 11

Linda and I weren't in Tennessee for the end of the filming. If there was a wrap party, I wasn't aware of it but I imagine there was. By then, I was deep into the final draft of a novel titled *Back to the Moon* and preparing for the publication of *Rocket Boys*. Word came that *Life* magazine was going publish an excerpt of the memoir and actor Beau Bridges had signed to narrate the audio version. International publishers in Great Britain, Spain, the Netherlands, Germany, Japan, Korea, Italy, France, China, and other countries were bidding for publishing rights. When Tom Spain faxed the *Rocket Boys* cover, I wasn't certain I liked it and Linda unreservedly hated it. It consisted of a stylized picket fence, the stakes made to look somewhat like rockets or perhaps the truncated stripes on a stylized American flag. My concern was the cover gave no hint what the story was within. When I told Tom I wanted a cover that showed some miner's kids holding a rocket with a mine tipple and mountains in the background, he said my concept was too literal. It would turn out that literal is sometimes good, especially when the book is something unique and difficult to describe in a few words.

Tom asked me to list celebrities I thought might be interested in the book. The one that came immediately to mind was David Letterman. Long before I had even thought about writing *Rocket Boys*, I'd taught David to scuba dive during a weekend in New York. At the time, I had used my NASA acumen to build an underwater space suit to train students at Space Camp in Huntsville. When Dave's producers found out about it, they flew me up to New York to teach him how to scuba dive and wear the suit, the idea to do an all underwater show. Although the show was never done, I figured Dave would remember who I was and might like what I'd written.

In July, Linda and I were flown out to Los Angeles to see a cut of the film with Chuck and Joe. It was the first time I'd seen the movie from beginning to end and I was surprised how well it moved. Joe and editor Robert Dalva had clearly done a great job, all the disjointed parts blending together perfectly. Joe's somber lighting effects, matching the actual sky for much of the shoot, had also proved to be perfect for the movie. There was also something else that was clearly established. This was Jake Gyllenhaal's movie. His performance was brilliant.

When the lights came up, I was feeling pleased. A representative from Universal Studios stood up and asked the test audience for their reaction and their comments showed they enthusiastically loved the movie. Then the Universal rep asked the audience if they liked the title. When the response was more or less a shrug, the questioner pressed until he got what I thought he wanted, that the title *Rocket Boys* wasn't the right title for this film. I got a sinking feeling in my stomach. Why an interest in a name change?

Afterwards, with Chuck and Joe both basking in the glow of the pleased audience, I kept my peace about the title, even though I thought it would be a disaster if the book was called one thing and the movie another. When I next talked to Chuck, he gave it to me straight. Universal marketing people didn't like *Rocket Boys* and were determined to change it for several good reasons. One of them was they felt my title was too similar to *The Rocketeer*, a previous Joe Johnston film. Another was they were afraid there might be confusion with a silly 1997 movie titled *RocketMan*. The third reason, and the one Chuck gave the most weight to, was Universal marketing executives thought the core audience for the film would be women over thirty and they were certain few in that demographic would want to go to a movie titled *Rocket Boys*. Although I understood the problem with the similar-sounding titles, I didn't believe the audience for our movie was going to be mostly women over thirty. Although I lobbied Chuck and Joe to head it off, I soon realized they had no stake in protecting the title. When I told him about the possible name change, Mickey told me Universal held the cards and if they wanted a change, it would be done. When I told Tom Spain, he was appalled. A couple of titles were floated past me. One was *Hearts in the Sky,* which made me want to throw up. When someone suggested *Homer Hickam*, I begged them not to do it. In my memoir, Homer Hickam was the father. It would be totally confusing.

Eventually, a title was found that satisfied everyone involved except me. It was Joe who came up with it by putting *Rocket Boys* in his computer and tasking it to give him an anagram. An anagram is when the letters of words are rearranged to make other words and the computer spat out the only anagram that made any sense: *October Sky.* This, as it happened, was the day Joe edited the scene in the movie where Homer looks up into the October sky and watches *Sputnik* fly over Coalwood. As soon as he saw it, Joe thought to himself: *This is way cosmic.* Immediately, he called Chuck who agreed it was way cosmic, indeed. Excited, they called me. When I heard the new title, I was somewhat less than thrilled but Chuck ignored my negativity. "Great!" he said. "We knew you'd love it!" Then he and Joe hung up.

All the misgivings I had about the movie came tumbling back. I called Mickey to complain but he said he liked the title. "They know what they're doing," he advised me for the umpteenth time. After the book was published, Joe would email me an explanation that further justified the change, saying when his sister saw *Rocket Boys* in the book store with its red, white, and blue star-spangled picket fence cover, she thought it was a book about military rockets. *October Sky* was the better title, he said, because it made people think about looking up. The poster Universal developed for the movie was also much closer to what I wanted for the book cover with Jake/Homer looking up at the moon and a mine tipple and mountains in the background.

*Rocket Boys* was published on October 16, 1998, and I had my first radio interview the same morning. The interviewer's first question was, "So, Hiram, why did you write this book about John Glenn?" For a moment, I froze. Not knowing my name didn't surprise me, but not being aware of the subject of the memoir did. I recovered as best I could. "I'm sure John Glenn will love the book," I said, "but this is the story of teenaged boys in the West Virginia coalfields who built rockets."

The sound I got back from the interviewer was crickets so I more or less interviewed myself until he pulled the plug. The next interviews were only a little better (mostly, my name was pronounced Hickman) but since none of the radio hosts had actually read the book, they instead asked questions about the space program which did nothing to sell the book. When I read Delacorte's promotional material sent to the stations, I saw it was mostly about me being a NASA engineer and not much about the story of the boys and people of Coalwood. It was almost as if my publisher lost its nerve at the last minute and decided to make *Rocket Boy*s a "space" book, whether it was or not. There was even a reference in the copy about Senator John Glenn flying aboard the shuttle. It was no wonder the interviewers were confused.

As book sales dribbled in, Tom called to report they were good but not great and my book tour was being extended to three months including a lot more radio and television. I hit the road again and, before long, sales for the book began to rise. Tom said it was probably because people were starting to talk about the book and recommending it to other readers. Independent booksellers were also enamored with it and were telling their customers that *Rocket Boys* was a great read.

In London, where I went to push the book for the UK publisher Fourth Estate, I came down with a terrible case of laryngitis. Unfortunately, that was when David Letterman told the publisher that he'd read *Rocket Boys*, loved it, and wanted me on his show right away. Unhappily, my voice was gone and it was impossible. Still, *Rocket Boys* was named by the New York Times as one of the "Notable Books of 1998" and also climbed to the paper's extended best-seller list. The reports from book stores country-wide was enthusiastic. The reviews on Amazon were consistently five stars. Progress was being made.

Delacorte flew me and Linda to New York for the National Book Critics Circle award and Tom and other executives accompanied us to the Tishman Auditorium for the announcement. I sought out Sylvia Nasar, the author of *A Beautiful Mind*, the book Tom said was my main competition. Ironically, it was the story of John Nash, a man from the West Virginia coalfields who grew up only thirty miles away from Coalwood. Nash, suffering from schizophrenia and paranoia, had gone on to win the Nobel Prize for economics. Although I hadn't read the book, everything I'd heard about it was good. I shook Nasar's hand and told her, with Tom standing beside me, "I hope you win. You deserve it."

When the announcement came that *A Beautiful Mind* was the winner, Tom provided me with a wan smile and said, "Well, you got your wish, Homer."

The movie apparently wasn't going to win any prizes, either. Originally scheduled to come out in December to make it eligible for the 1998 Academy Awards, Universal instead pushed it back to February, traditionally a dump month for films. When I talked to Mickey about it, he said, "No matter when it comes out, it's still a great movie." This was little consolation considering how hard everybody had worked on it.

Then, Tom called to tell me Delacorte had decided to bring *Rocket Boys* out as a mass market paperback under the Dell label retitled *October Sky* to coincide with the movie release. I could tell by his tight voice that he was upset with this decision. "The title change is just the mass market," he reassured me. "We'll keep the hardcover with the old title and later we'll bring out a trade paperback titled *Rocket Boys*, too."

Everything seemed to be going wrong, but Linda told me to stop worrying because it was out of my hands. Happily, book sales rose as the Christmas season approached and great reviews were still pouring in from all over the country. A lot of complimentary letters and email were also reaching me. Before long, we started talking about a website that we eventually developed for all my books (http://www.homerhickam.com).

The Hollywood premiere of the movie was on my 56th birthday, Feb. 19, 1999. A limo picked me and Linda up at our hotel and we rode with Jake, Naomi, and Mickey. Mickey looked over at me and said, "Savor this moment, Homer. It will never come again."

In fact, I did savor it. Linda was dressed to the nines and looked stunning. Jake was so excited he could hardly sit still. We waited until he did his turn down the red carpet, then followed as cameras flashed and people cheered as if we were somebody important. The movie was shown to tremendous applause and a standing ovation. When the lights came on, I got my first indication that the movie was going to touch the hearts, minds, souls, and guts of a lot of people. At the party afterwards, Pete Conrad, the third man to walk on the moon, sought me out to tell me how much he'd loved the movie. It was an amazing moment.

The second premiere was in Knoxville, close to the locations where *October Sky* was filmed. My mom and brother Jim were able to attend this one along with all the surviving Rocket Boys. Nearly all the extras showed up as well, carrying with them souvenirs of the movie including some of the rockets. How they got them, I have no idea but I didn't ask

100

any questions. Jake was there along with Scott Miles and, of course, Joe and Chuck. Of the two premieres, the one in Knoxville was a lot more fun. The extras in attendance were so excited about *their* movie. You could just feel their love during the screening. It was contagious.

Finally, I got my chance to go on *Letterman*, this time to talk about both the book and the movie. Dave and I had a great time and then he showed a clip of me teaching him to scuba dive rather than a clip of the movie. Universal didn't much like that but it was Dave's show and I didn't mind. In any case, it didn't much matter. Review after review proclaimed *October Sky* as a fresh and inspirational film and, probably as a result, book sales surged. Within a few days, the mass market was number one on the New York Times best-seller list. Tom and I were both thrilled by this because the movie had helped the book reach an audience it might never have found.

Interestingly, despite the prodigious reviews, *October Sky* didn't fare so well at the box office. Although it had an initial surge of popularity, it quickly faded in U.S. theaters. This was alleviated somewhat when we traveled to Italy for the Venice Film Festival and then the London Film Festival. In both cases, the movie was met with critical success and standing ovations. In Venice, the audience even turned around to enthusiastically cheer Joe, Chuck, me, and Laura Dern. Laura was so excited by their reaction that she kissed my hand. No one was more surprised than me but it was heartfelt and I thought she had done a magnificent job as Miss Riley. In the final edit, nearly every change she had insisted upon to make her character stronger and closer to the real Miss Riley had ultimately been adopted. I was proud and happy for her.

Linda and I also got to know Chris Cooper much better during our sojourn to Venice. He and his wife, Marianne, also an accomplished actor, revealed to Linda and me that it was their first vacation together since their son Jesse had been born with cerebral palsy. We came to love

101

them and their quiet courage in support of their son. We also got to have a lot of fun exploring Venice together!

Venice was also our chance to get to know Chuck and Lynda Gordon better. Chuck's brother Lawrence and his wife were also attending the festival. Although we were all busy giving interviews and otherwise interacting with the media and festival participants, we had one evening together at a nice cellar restaurant. Properly wined and dined, we talked about everything and nothing until Linda and I felt as if we'd known both sets of Gordons forever. They could not possibly have been more gracious and kind. Joe and Lisa Johnston were also with us. Lisa was and is a sweet woman, filled with pride for Joe's accomplishments and it was wonderful to visit with her. The reception the Italians gave Joe's movie was clearly very pleasing to him. It was nice to see him relaxed and happy after the grueling days he'd spent making it.

*October Sky* got a similar reception in London, the audience responding with endless applause that belied the usual English reserve. One of the best aspects of both the Venice and London film festivals was that Linda and I, because of scheduling necessities, got to fly back to the states aboard the Concorde twice. It was an amazing aircraft that allowed us to see the curvature of the Earth, something Sonny Hickam would have been astonished to see and so was Homer Hickam (Jr.), the grown-up who'd taken his place.

There was one more gathering we would all have together, this time with writer Lewis Colick in attendance. In May, Chuck called and asked us to come out to Los Angeles to attend the Humanitas Prize luncheon. This award was conceived by Ellwood Keiser, a Roman Catholic priest famous within the Hollywood community as "Father Bud." His idea was to honor screenplay writers for scripts that best promoted "human dignity, meaning, and freedom." *Good Will Hunting* had won the previous year. *The Shawshank Redemption* and *Schindler's List* were also winners. Chuck explained to me that it was a big deal in Hollywood for a writer to win it. I was pleased that Lewis was in the running but I saw he was up against *Saving Private Ryan*, one of the most popular movies ever made. Also nominated was *A Civil Action*, a successful John Travolta vehicle based on a book that won the National Book Critics Circle award. It was therefore all the more astonishing when the announcement came that Lewis Colick for *October Sky* was the winner. Although I had doubted his original script and some of his interpretations of my characters, it was confirmation that Lewis was a great writer. As he rose to receive his prize, I embraced this truth.

Linda and I flew home, pleased with how everything had turned out and ready to take on whatever came next. I sensed my great literary and movie adventure was essentially over. After all, the movie was out of the theaters, the book had receded from the New York Times best-seller lists, and I was now deep into my next book and looking forward to writing more.

But were *Rocket Boys* and *October Sky* really over?

What I didn't know, what nobody knew, was that there was very much yet to come.

FROM ROCKET BOYS TO OCTOBER SKY

## 12

There was a pause, almost as if everyone was taking a breath. After *Back to the Moon*, I got busy writing *The Coalwood Way*, a Christmas story I'd pulled from the original memoir. I also had in mind to write historical fiction. During the research and writing of *Torpedo Junction*, some great stories had come to me about the people of the fabled Outer Banks of North Carolina. There was good novel there just waiting to be written, I was certain of it.

Then it began. The letters and emails. The interviews. The requests for appearances and speeches from every state and nearly every country around the world. Everyone, it seemed, had fallen in love with the real Rocket Boys, whether they knew us from my book or from the movie. Frank Weimann took me across New York to the offices of Greater Talent Network, a lecture agency, and signed me up. Before long, I was back out on the road, this time making speeches and telling stories. No matter what I wanted to talk about, what people wanted to hear most were my tales of Coalwood, my parents, and boyhood dreams. Happily, I discovered my West Virginia roots had provided me with the ability to tell a good story in front of a crowd. When people came to see me, I knew they thought I would be technical and dry and were always surprised to find I soon had them laughing and sometimes crying. After all, the stories I had to tell had the bittersweet ending of my father and little Sonny together on that ancient slack dump. I often read from *Rocket*

*Boys* of that moment and there was rarely a dry eye in the house, including my own. Those times still live within me. In the epilogue of *Rocket Boys*, I wrote this:

> *Sometimes, now, I wake at night, thinking I have heard the sound of my father's footsteps on the stairs, or the shuffling boots and low murmur of the hoot-owl shift going to work. In that half-world between sleep and wakefulness, I can almost hear the ringing of a hammer on steel and the dry hiss of the arc welder at the little machine shop by the tipple. But it is only a trick of my imagination; nearly everything that I knew in Coalwood is gone . . . Yet, I believe for those of us who keep it in our hearts, Coalwood still lives . . . Even now, Coalwood endures, and no one, nor careless industry or overzealous government, can ever completely destroy it—not while we who once lived there may recall our life among its places, or especially remember rockets that once leapt into the air, propelled not by physics but by the vibrant love of an honorable people, and the instruction of a dear teacher, and the dreams of boys.*

Gradually, we realized that *Rocket Boys* (or its mass market paperback version retitled *October Sky*) was being taught in classrooms by both science and English/Literature teachers. When so many emails came in from students asking for detailed information about the book, Linda and I figured out they were asking for help with their homework! For assistance, we added resources to www.homerhickam.com for both teachers and students. A lot of the email was also about the movie, too. It was being shown in schools everywhere, not only in the USA, but across the world. I began to use the line, "Every substitute teacher in the world shows *October Sky*." I think it's nearly true. From our mail, it was clear that a lot of teachers were using both the book and movie. Some schools had Rocket Boys celebrations where the students dressed up like characters in the book. At one school where I visited, I was delighted to be met by a huddle of "Dorothy Plunks" and "Valentines," dressed in poodle skirts and sweaters!

Awards began to roll in, so many I began to lose track, even including an honorary doctorate from West Virginia's Marshall University. *Rocket Boys/October Sky* also began to be picked by communities and libraries across the country as their annual read. So many of them picked the book, a search on the Internet revealed that it was the most frequently selected book during the first decade of the 21st Century, even ahead of *To Kill a Mockingbird*. Pretty soon, the memoir was being hailed as a classic. I was savvy enough to know that writers who write classics are sometimes pigeonholed by that work forever and that happened to me to an extent. Even though I was writing about one book a year, people who met me invariably said, "Oh, Mr. Hickam, I love your *book*!" and I needed no explanation as to which book they were talking about. Of course, most writers would be delighted to write a book that is beloved by millions and I am no exception.

The popularity of the book and movie continues to grow. The film is shown regularly in classrooms and on network and cable television world-wide. I always know where it's being shown by the flood of email we receive from India, Brazil, Iraq, China or wherever. Thousands of emails and letters from students determined to go into engineering and science stream into our home. They invariably tell me it's because of the inspiration they've received from the movie or the book. Others write to simply say thank you for a story that touched their hearts. When I made a speech at the U. S. Air Force Academy, a group of cadets sought me out to tell me they were there because of *October Sky*. I was thrilled then, and still am.

One of the best things that happened because of the popularity of the book and the movie was the focus that turned on little Coalwood. After the mine closed in 1978, houses there were abandoned or torn down, the old school was burned to the ground, the company offices and machine shops were left to rot, and the people in the town found

themselves mostly unemployed. With a new spirit provided by the story
of their Rocket Boys, Coalwood rallied and began to put on an annual
October Sky Festival. For thirteen years, the remaining Rocket Boys and
I went to Coalwood and there signed books all day while people flocked
from everywhere to celebrate our story and the history of the coalfields.
When there were too few people left in Coalwood to put the festival on,
the city of Beckley, West Virginia, picked it up, renaming it the Rocket
Boys Festival (www.rocketboysfestival.com). The other Rocket Boys and I
continue to support it because it brings people to southern West Virginia
to celebrate our coal mining heritage.

Another marvelous result of the story's popularity was the creation
of a Broadway-style musical based on the book. Titled *Rocket Boys The
Musical*, it was co-written by me and Carl Anthony Tramon, with music
and lyrics by Dan Tramon and Diana Belkowski. The musical has now
settled into an annual staging at Theatre West Virginia and we hope it
will eventually go to Broadway.

After *The Coalwood Way*, which climbed to the New York Times
best-sellers list, Tom Spain left Delacorte and I lost my best friend within
the Bantam Doubleday Dell (BDD) empire. *Sky of Stone* was my next
memoir and of the three memoirs I wrote, I thought it was the best
written. Unfortunately, it was released immediately after the 9/11
attacks on New York and Washington and struggled to find its audience
in the aftermath. Still, it has turned into one of those books with a long
career of sales and affection.

As soon as I got home from the *Sky of Stone* tour, Frank called to
say that Health Communications, the company that publishes the
*Chicken Soup for the Soul* books, wanted me to write a book to encourage
the American people to go forward and overcome fear. The result was *We
Are Not Afraid* that told stories about how the people of Coalwood
overcame fear and the various disasters inevitable in a coal town. When

Frank asked me what I wanted to write next, I told him my idea to write what would become *The Keeper's Son* and we signed with Thomas Dunne of St. Martin's. The next three novels were my "Josh Thurlow" series which was then followed by *The Dinosaur Hunter*, a mystery set in the fossil grounds and badlands of Montana. Although none of these novels became huge best-sellers, they gathered a core of readers who looked forward to my work past *Rocket Boys*. Frank soon brought me together with another publisher, Thomas Nelson, which published *Red Helmet*, a novel of romance in the modern West Virginia coalfields, followed by the Helium-3 series set on the moon 120 years in the future that includes *Crater, Crescent*, and, in 2014, *Crater Trueblood and the Lunar Rescue Company*. After these novels, I am planning to write for William Morrow a humorous tale of my parents when they were young and carried Mom's pet alligator from the hills of West Virginia back to its swampy home in Florida. It will be different from anything I've written before and that, for me, is one of its appeals. I love a good challenge.

Chuck Gordon and Joe Johnston remain good friends and we often talk or see each other. Mickey Freiberg continued working in Hollywood on my behalf to the day he died in 2012. Through his efforts, *Back to the Moon* was optioned several times by different producers, and *Sky of Stone* by Hallmark. *The Keeper's Son* received an option and there was a lot of interest in *Red Helmet*. Yet, for one reason or another, none of these books made it all the way to the coveted Hollywood green light. It reinforced all the more how special and miraculous the writing of *Rocket Boys* and the making of *October Sky* were. All that I can conclude is there was a greater force behind their success. That's why I wrote this in the conclusion of *Sky of Stone*:

*As for me, I hope to continue writing and entertaining my readers, and maybe even providing some occasional illumination on life as it was, is, or shall be. I am a lucky man and I know it. The Engineer of the Universe has looked after this Coalwood boy, don't ask me why. The wheel of Jeremiah continues to turn with those great hands on it, shaping me, shaping us all. There are miracles everywhere, although sometimes they are concealed, not by God, but by our own eyes. All we need to do is look, and they will be seen.*